THE DEHUMANIZATION OF ART
AND
NOTES ON THE NOVEL

THE DEHUMANIZATION OF ART AND NOTES ON THE NOVEL

BY JOSÉ ORTEGA Y GASSET

TRANSLATED BY HELENE WEYL

PRINCETON UNIVERSITY PRESS, 1948

PRINCETON, NEW JERSEY

✧

This book is a translation of
La Deshumanización del arte e Ideas sobre la Novela.
The Spanish original was published by
Revista de Occidente, Madrid, 1925

PRINTED IN THE UNITED STATES OF AMERICA
BY PRINCETON UNIVERSITY PRESS AT PRINCETON, NEW JERSEY

CONTENTS

THE
DEHUMANIZATION
OF ART

"Non creda donna Berta e ser Martino . . ."
—DIVINA COMMEDIA, PARADISO, XIII

*A*mong the many excellent, though inadequately developed, ideas of the eminent French philosopher J. M. Guyau we must count his intention to study art from a sociological point of view.* The subject may at first appear unprofitable. Approaching art from the side of its social effects looks very much like putting the cart before the horse, or studying a man by his shadow. The social effects of art seem such an accidental thing, so remote from the aesthetic essence that it does not quite appear how, starting from them, we can ever hope to penetrate into the inner frame of styles. Guyau doubtless failed to make the best of his ingenious idea. His short life and tragic rushing toward death prevented him from clarifying his insight and distinguishing the obvious aspects from the hidden but more relevant ones. We may almost say that of his book *Art from a Sociological Point of View* only the title exists; the rest is yet to be written.

The fruitfulness of a sociology of art was revealed to me unexpectedly when, a few years ago, I wrote a brief study on the new epoch in music which begins with Debussy.† My purpose was to define as clearly as possible the difference of style between the new music and traditional music. The problem was strictly aesthetic, and yet it turned out that the shortest way of tackling it

* Jean Marie Guyau, *L'art au point de vue sociologique.* Paris: F. Alcan, 1897.

† Cf. the author's essay "Musicalia" in *El Espectador* (Madrid: Calpe, 1921), vol. III, 25.

started from a sociological fact: the unpopularity of the new music.

In the following I will speak more in general and consider all the arts that are still somewhat alive in the Western world—that is, not only music, but also painting, poetry, and the theater. It is amazing how compact a unity every historical epoch presents throughout its various manifestations. One and the same inspiration, one and the same biological style, are recognizable in the several branches of art. The young musician—himself unaware of it—strives to realize in his medium the same aesthetic values as his contemporary colleagues— the poet, the painter, the playwright—in theirs. And this identity of artistic purpose necessarily produces identical sociological consequences. In fact, the unpopularity of the new music has its counterpart in a similar unpopularity of the other Muses. All modern art is unpopular, and it is so not accidentally and by chance, but essentially and by fate.

It might be said that every newcomer among styles passes through a stage of quarantine. The battle of *Hernani* comes to mind, and all the other skirmishes connected with the advent of Romanticism. However, the unpopularity of present-day art is of a different kind. A distinction must be made between what is not popular and what is unpopular. A new style takes some time in winning popularity; it is not popular, but it is not unpopular either. The break-through of Romanticism, although a frequently cited example, is, as a sociological phenomenon, exactly the opposite of the present situation of art. Romanticism was very quick in winning "the people" to whom the old classical art had never appealed. The enemy with whom Romanticism had to fight it out was precisely a select minority irretrievably sold to the classical forms of the *"ancien régime"* in poetry. The works of the romanticists were the first, after the invention of printing, to enjoy large editions. Romanticism was the prototype of a popular style. First-born of democracy, it was coddled by the masses.

Modern art, on the other hand, will always have the masses against it. It is essentially unpopular; moreover, it is antipopular. Any of its works automatically produces a curious effect on the general public. It divides the public into two groups: one very small, formed by those who are favorably inclined towards it; another very large—the hostile majority. (Let us ignore that ambiguous fauna—the snobs.) Thus the work of art acts like a social agent which segregates from the shapeless mass of the many two different castes of men.

Which is the differentiating principle that creates these two antagonistic groups? Every work of art arouses differences of opinion. Some like it, some don't; some like it more, some like it less. Such disagreements have no organic character, they are not a matter of principles. A person's chance disposition determines on which side he will fall. But in the case of the new art the split occurs in a deeper layer than that on which differences of personal taste reside. It is not that the majority does not *like* the art of the young and the minority likes it, but that the majority, the masses, do not *understand* it. The old bigwigs who were present at the performance of *Hernani* understood Victor Hugo's play very well; precisely because they understood it they disliked it. Faithfully adhering to definite aesthetic norms, they were disgusted at the new artistic values which this piece of art proposed to them.

"From a sociological point of view" the characteristic feature of the new art is, in my judgment, that it divides the public into the two classes of those who understand it and those who do not. This implies that one group possesses an organ of comprehension denied to the other—that they are two different varieties of the human species. The new art obviously addresses itself not to everybody, as did Romanticism, but to a specially gifted minority. Hence the indignation it arouses in the masses. When a man dislikes a work of art, but understands it, he feels superior to it; and there is no reason for indignation. But when his dislike is due to his failure to understand, he feels vaguely humiliated and this rankling sense of inferiority must be counterbalanced by indignant self-assertion. Through its mere presence, the art of the young compels the average citizen to realize that he is just this—the average citizen, a creature incapable of receiving the sacrament of art, blind and deaf to pure beauty. But such a thing cannot be done after a hundred years of adulation of the masses and apotheosis of the people. Accustomed to ruling supreme, the masses feel that the new art, which is the art of a privileged aristocracy of finer senses, endangers their

rights as men. Whenever the new Muses present themselves, the masses bristle.

For a century and a half the masses have claimed to
be the whole of society. Stravinski's music or Pirandello's drama have the sociological effect of compelling
the people to recognize itself for what it is: a component
among others of the social structure, inert matter of the
historical process, a secondary factor in the cosmos of
spiritual life. On the other hand, the new art also helps
the elite to recognize themselves and one another in the
drab mass of society and to learn their mission which
consists in being few and holding their own against the
many.

A time must come in which society, from politics to
art, reorganizes itself into two orders or ranks: the illustrious and the vulgar. That chaotic, shapeless, and un-
differentiated state without discipline and social structure in which Europe has lived these hundred and fifty
years cannot go on. Behind all contemporary life lurks
the provoking and profound injustice of the assumption
that men are actually equal. Each move among men so
obviously reveals the opposite that each move results in
a painful clash.

If this subject were broached in politics the passions
aroused would run too high to make oneself understood. Fortunately the aforementioned unity of spirit
within a historical epoch allows us to point out serenely
and with perfect clarity in the germinating art of our
time the same symptoms and signals of a moral revision

that in politics present themselves obscured by low passions.

"Nolite fieri," the evangelist exhorts us, *"sicut equus et mulus quibus non est intellectus"*—do not act like horses and mules that lack understanding. The masses kick and do not understand. Let us try to do better and to extract from modern art its essential principle. That will enable us to see in what profound sense modern art is unpopular.

ARTISTIC ART

(If the new art is not accessible to every man this implies that its impulses are not of a generically human kind. It is an art not for men in general but for a special class of men who may not be better but who evidently are different.

One point must be clarified before we go on. What is it the majority of people call aesthetic pleasure? What happens in their minds when they "like" a work of art; for instance, a theatrical performance? The answer is easy. A man likes a play when he has become interested in the human destinies presented to him, when the love and hatred, the joys and sorrows of the personages so move his heart that he participates in it all as though it were happening in real life. And he calls a work "good" if it succeeds in creating the illusion necessary to make the imaginary personages appear like living persons. In poetry he seeks the passion and pain of the man behind the poet. Paintings attract him if he finds on them figures of men or women whom it would be interesting to meet. A landscape is pronounced "pretty" if the country it represents deserves for its loveliness or its grandeur to be visited on a trip.

It thus appears that to the majority of people aesthetic pleasure means a state of mind which is essentially undistinguishable from their ordinary behavior. It differs merely in accidental qualities, being perhaps less utilitarian, more intense, and free from painful consequences. But the object towards which their attention and, consequently, all their other mental activities are directed is the same as in daily life: people and passions. By art they understand a means through which they are brought in contact with interesting human affairs. Artistic forms proper—figments, fantasy— are tolerated only if they do not interfere with the perception of human forms and fates. As soon as purely aesthetic elements predominate and the story of John and Mary grows elusive, most people feel out of their depth and are at a loss what to make of the scene, the book, or the painting. As they have never practiced any other attitude but the practical one in which a man's feelings are aroused and he is emotionally involved, a work that does not invite sentimental intervention leaves them without a cue.

Now, this is a point which has to be made perfectly clear. Not only is grieving and rejoicing at such human destinies as a work of art presents or narrates a very different thing from true artistic pleasure, but preoccupation with the human content of the work is in principle incompatible with aesthetic enjoyment proper.

We have here a very simple optical problem. To see a thing we must adjust our visual apparatus in a certain way. If the adjustment is inadequate the thing is seen indistinctly or not at all. Take a garden seen through a window. Looking at the garden we adjust our eyes in such a way that the ray of vision travels through the pane without delay and rests on the shrubs and flowers. Since we are focusing on the garden and our ray of vision is directed toward it, we do not see the window but look clear through it. The purer the glass, the less we see it. But we can also deliberately disregard the garden and, withdrawing the ray of vision, detain it at the window. We then lose sight of the garden; what we still behold of it is a confused mass of color which appears pasted to the pane. Hence to see the garden and to see the windowpane are two incompatible operations which exclude one another because they require different adjustments.

Similarly a work of art vanishes from sight for a beholder who seeks in it nothing but the moving fate of John and Mary or Tristan and Isolde and adjusts his vision to this. Tristan's sorrows are sorrows and can evoke compassion only in so far as they are taken as real. But an object of art is artistic only in so far as it is not real. In order to enjoy Titian's portrait of Charles the Fifth on horseback we must forget that this is Charles the Fifth in person and see instead a portrait—that is, an image, a fiction. The portrayed person and his portrait are two entirely different things; we are interested in either one or the other. In the first case we "live" with Charles the Fifth, in the second we look at an object of art.

But not many people are capable of adjusting their perceptive apparatus to the pane and the transparency that is the work of art. Instead they look right through it and revel in the human reality with which the work deals. When they are invited to let go of this prey and to direct their attention to the work of art itself they will say that they cannot see such a thing, which indeed they cannot, because it is all artistic transparency and without substance.

During the nineteenth century artists proceeded in all too impure a fashion. They reduced the strictly aesthetic elements to a minimum and let the work consist almost entirely in a fiction of human realities. In this sense all normal art of the last century must be called realistic. Beethoven and Wagner were realistic, and so was Chateaubriand as well as Zola. Seen from the vantage-point of our day Romanticism and Naturalism draw closer together and reveal their common realistic root.

Works of this kind are only partially works of art, or artistic objects. Their enjoyment does not depend upon our power to focus on transparencies and images, a power characteristic of the artistic sensibility; all they require is human sensibility and willingness to sympathize with our neighbor's joys and worries. No wonder that nineteenth century art has been so popular; it is made for the masses inasmuch as it is not art but an extract from life. Let us remember that in epochs with two different types of art, one for minorities and one for the majority, the latter has always been realistic.*

I will not now discuss whether pure art is possible. Perhaps it is not; but as the reasons that make me inclined to think so are somewhat long and difficult the subject better be dropped. Besides, it is not of major importance for the matter in hand. Even though pure art may be impossible there doubtless can prevail a tendency toward a purification of art. Such a tendency would effect a progressive elimination of the human, all too human, elements predominant in romantic and naturalistic production. And in this process a point can be reached in which the human content has grown so thin that it is negligible. We then have an art which can be comprehended only by people possessed of the peculiar gift of artistic sensibility—an art for artists and not for the masses, for "quality" and not for hoi polloi.

That is why modern art divides the public into two classes, those who understand it and those who do not understand it—that is to say, those who are artists and those who are not. The new art is an artistic art.

I do not propose to extol the new way in art or to condemn the old. My purpose is to characterize them as the zoologist characterizes two contrasting species. The new art is a world-wide fact. For about twenty years now

* For instance in the Middle Ages. In accordance with the division of society in the two strata of noblemen and commoners, there existed an aristocratic art which was "conventional" and "idealistic," and a popular art which was realistic and satirical.

the most alert young people of two successive generations—in Berlin, Paris, London, New York, Rome, Madrid—have found themselves faced with the undeniable fact that they have no use for traditional art; moreover, that they detest it. With these young people one can do one of two things: shoot them, or try to understand them. As soon as one decides in favor of the latter it appears that they are endowed with a perfectly clear, coherent, and rational sense of art. Far from being a whim, their way of feeling represents the inevitable and fruitful result of all previous artistic achievement. Whimsical, arbitrary, and consequently unprofitable it would be to set oneself against the new style and obstinately remain shut up in old forms that are exhausted and the worse for wear. In art, as in morals, what ought to be done does not depend on our personal judgment; we have to accept the imperative imposed by the time. Obedience to the order of the day is the most hopeful choice open to the individual. Even so he may achieve nothing; but he is much more likely to fail if he insists on composing another Wagnerian opera, another naturalistic novel.

In art repetition is nothing. Each historical style can engender a certain number of different forms within a generic type. But there always comes a day when the magnificent mine is worked out. Such, for instance, has been the fate of the romantico-naturalistic novel and theater. It is a naïve error to believe that the present infecundity of these two genres is due to lack of talent. What happens is that the possible combinations within these literary forms are exhausted. It must be deemed fortunate that this situation coincides with the emergence of a new artistic sensibility capable of detecting other untouched veins.

When we analyze the new style we find that it contains certain closely connected tendencies. It tends (1) to dehumanize art, (2) to avoid living forms, (3) to see to it that the work of art is nothing but a work of art, (4) to consider art as play and nothing else, (5) to be essentially ironical, (6) to beware of sham and hence to aspire to scrupulous realization, (7) to regard art as a thing of no transcending consequence.

In the following I shall say a few words about each of these features of modern art.

A FEW DROPS OF PHENOMENOLOGY

(A great man is dying. His wife is by his bedside. A doctor takes the dying man's pulse. In the background two more persons are discovered: a reporter who is present for professional reasons, and a painter whom mere chance has brought here. Wife, doctor, reporter, and painter witness one and the same event. Nonetheless, this identical event—a man's death—impresses each of them in a different way. So different indeed that the several aspects have hardly anything in common. What this scene means to the wife who is all grief has so little to do with what it means to the painter who looks on impassively that it seems doubtful whether the two can be said to be present at the same event.

It thus becomes clear that one and the same reality may split up into many diverse realities when it is beheld from different points of view. And we cannot help asking ourselves: Which of all these realities must then be regarded as the real and authentic one? The answer, no matter how we decide, cannot but be arbitrary. Any preference can be founded on caprice only. All these realities are equivalent, each being authentic for its corresponding point of view. All we can do is to classify the points of view and to determine which among them seems, in a practical way, most normal or most spontaneous. Thus we arrive at a conception of reality that is by no means absolute, but at least practical and normative.

As for the points of view of the four persons present at the deathbed, the clearest means of distinguishing them is by measuring one of their dimensions, namely the emotional distance between each person and the event they all witness. For the wife of the dying man the distance shrinks to almost nothing. What is happening so tortures her soul and absorbs her mind that it becomes one with her person. Or to put it inversely, the wife is drawn into the scene, she is part of it. A thing can be seen, an event can be observed, only when we have separated it from ourselves and it has ceased to form a living part of our being. Thus the wife is not present at the scene, she is in it. She does not behold it, she "lives" it.

The doctor is several degrees removed. To him this is a professional case. He is not drawn into the event with the frantic and blinding anxiety of the poor woman. However it is his bounden duty as a doctor to take a serious interest, he carries responsibility, perhaps his professional honor is at stake. Hence he too, albeit in a less integral and less intimate way, takes part in the event. He is involved in it not with his heart but with the professional portion of his self. He too "lives" the scene although with an agitation originating not in the emotional center, but in the professional surface, of his existence.

When we now put ourselves in the place of the reporter we realize that we have traveled a long distance away from the tragic event. So far indeed that we have lost all emotional contact with it. The reporter, like the doctor, has been brought here for professional reasons and not out of a spontaneous human interest. But while the doctor's profession requires him to interfere, the reporter's requires him precisely to stay aloof; he has to confine himself to observing. To him the event is a mere scene, a pure spectacle on which he is expected to report in his newspaper column. He takes no feeling part in what is happening here, he is emotionally free, an outsider. He does not "live" the scene, he observes it. Yet he observes it with a view to telling his readers about it. He wants to interest them, to move them, and if possible to make them weep as though they each had been the dying man's best friend. From his schooldays he remembers Horace's recipe: *"Si vis me flere dolendum est primum ipsi tibi"*—if you want me to weep you must first grieve yourself.

Obedient to Horace the reporter is anxious to pretend emotion, hoping that it will benefit his literary performance. If he does not "live" the scene he at least pretends to "live" it.

The painter, in fine, completely unconcerned, does nothing but keep his eyes open. What is happening here is none of his business; he is, as it were, a hundred miles removed from it. His is a purely perceptive attitude; indeed, he fails to perceive the event in its entirety. The tragic inner meaning escapes his attention which is directed exclusively toward the visual part—color values, lights, and shadows. In the painter we find a maximum of distance and a minimum of feeling intervention.

The inevitable dullness of this analysis will, I hope, be excused if it now enables us to speak in a clear and precise way of a scale of emotional distances between ourselves and reality. In this scale, the degree of closeness is equivalent to the degree of feeling participation; the degree of remoteness, on the other hand, marks the degree to which we have freed ourselves from the real event, thus objectifying it and turning it into a theme of pure observation. At one end of the scale the world—persons, things, situations—is given to us in the aspect of "lived" reality; at the other end we see everything in the aspect of "observed" reality.

At this point we must make a remark that is essential in aesthetics and without which neither old art nor new art can be satisfactorily analyzed. Among the diverse aspects of reality we find one from which all the others derive and which they all presuppose: "lived" reality. If nobody had ever "lived" in pure and frantic abandonment a man's death, the doctor would not bother, the readers would not understand the reporter's pathos, and the canvas on which the painter limned a person on a bed surrounded by mourning figures would be meaningless. The same holds for any object, be it a person, a thing, or a situation. The primal aspect of an apple is that in which I see it when I am about to eat it. All its other possible forms—when it appears, for instance, in a Baroque ornament, or on a still life of Cézanne's, or in the eternal metaphor of a girl's apple cheeks—preserve more or less that original aspect. A painting or a poem without any vestiges of "lived" forms would be unintelligible, i.e., nothing—as a discourse is nothing whose every word is emptied of its customary meaning.

That is to say, in the scale of realities "lived" reality holds a peculiar primacy which compels us to regard it as "the" reality. Instead of "lived" reality we may say "human" reality. The painter who impassively witnesses the death scene appears "inhuman." In other words, the human point of view is that in which we "live" situations, persons, things. And, vice versa, realities—a woman, a countryside, an event—are human when they present the aspect in which they are usually "lived."

As an example, the importance of which will appear later, let us mention that among the realities which constitute the world are our ideas. We use our ideas in a "human" way when we employ them for thinking things. Thinking of Napoleon, for example, we are normally concerned with the great man of that name. A psychologist, on the other hand, adopts an unusual, "inhuman" attitude when he forgets about Napoleon and, prying into his own mind, tries to analyze his idea of Napoleon as such idea. His perspective is the opposite of that prevailing in spontaneous life. The idea, instead of functioning as the means to think an object with, is itself made the object and the aim of thinking. We shall soon see the unexpected use which the new art has made of this "inhuman" inversion.

FIRST INSTALLMENT ON THE DEHUMANIZATION OF ART

❨ With amazing swiftness modern art has split up into a multitude of divergent directions. Nothing is easier than to stress the differences. But such an emphasis on the distinguishing and specific features would be pointless without a previous account of the common fund that in a varying and sometimes contradictory manner asserts itself throughout modern art. Did not Aristotle already observe that things differ in what they have in common? Because all bodies are colored we notice that they are differently colored. Species are nothing if not modifications of a genus, and we cannot understand them unless we realize that they draw, in their several ways, upon a common patrimony.

I am little interested in special directions of modern

art and, but for a few exceptions, even less in special works. Nor do I, for that matter, expect anybody to be particularly interested in my valuation of the new artistic produce. Writers who have nothing to convey but their praise or dispraise of works of art had better abstain from writing. They are unfit for this arduous task.

The important thing is that there unquestionably exists in the world a new artistic sensibility.* Over against the multiplicity of special directions and individual works, the new sensibility represents the generic fact and the source, as it were, from which the former spring. This sensibility it is worth while to define. And when we seek to ascertain the most general and most characteristic feature of modern artistic production we come upon the tendency to dehumanize art. After what we have said above, this formula now acquires a tolerably precise meaning.

Let us compare a painting in the new style with one of, say, 1860. The simplest procedure will be to begin by setting against one another the objects they represent: a man perhaps, a house, or a mountain. It then appears that the artist of 1860 wanted nothing so much as to give to the objects in his picture the same looks and airs they possess outside it when they occur as parts of the "lived" or "human" reality. Apart from this he may have been animated by other more intricate aesthetic

* This new sensibility is a gift not only of the artist proper but also of his audience. When I said above that the new art is an art for artists I understood by "artists" not only those who produce this art but also those who are capable of perceiving purely artistic values.

ambitions, but what interests us is that his first concern was with securing this likeness. Man, house, mountain are at once recognized, they are our good old friends; whereas on a modern painting we are at a loss to recognize them. It might be supposed that the modern painter has failed to achieve resemblance. But then some pictures of the 1860's are "poorly" painted, too, and the objects in them differ considerably from the corresponding objects outside them. And yet, whatever the differences, the very blunders of the traditional artist point toward the "human" object; they are downfalls on the way toward it and somehow equivalent to the orienting words "This is a cock" with which Cervantes lets the painter Orbanejo enlighten his public. In modern paintings the opposite happens. It is not that the painter is bungling and fails to render the natural (natural = human) thing because he deviates from it, but that these deviations point in a direction opposite to that which would lead to reality.

Far from going more or less clumsily toward reality, the artist is seen going against it. He is brazenly set on deforming reality, shattering its human aspect, dehumanizing it. With the things represented on traditional paintings we could have imaginary intercourse. Many a young Englishman has fallen in love with Gioconda. With the objects of modern pictures no intercourse is possible. By divesting them of their aspect of "lived" reality the artist has blown up the bridges and burned the ships that could have taken us back to our daily world. He leaves us locked up in an abstruse universe, surrounded by objects with which human dealings are inconceivable, and thus compels us to improvise other forms of intercourse completely distinct from our ordinary ways with things. We must invent unheard-of gestures to fit those singular figures. This new way of life which presupposes the annulment of spontaneous life is precisely what we call understanding and enjoyment of art. Not that this life lacks sentiments and passions, but those sentiments and passions evidently belong to a flora other than that which covers the hills and dales of primary and human life. What those ultra-objects* evoke in our inner artist are secondary passions, specifically aesthetic sentiments.

It may be said that, to achieve this result, it would be simpler to dismiss human forms—man, house, mountain—altogether and to construct entirely original figures. But, in the first place, this is not feasible.† Even in the most abstract ornamental line a stubborn reminiscence lurks of certain "natural" forms. Secondly— and this is the crucial point—the art of which we speak is inhuman not only because it contains no things human, but also because it is an explicit act of dehumanization. In his escape from the human world the young artist cares less for the "*terminus ad quem*," the startling fauna at which he arrives, than for the "*terminus a quo*," the human aspect which he destroys. The question is not to paint something altogether different from

* "Ultraism" is one of the most appropriate names that have been coined to denote the new sensibility.

† An attempt has been made in this extreme sense—in certain works by Picasso—but it has failed signally.

a man, a house, a mountain, but to paint a man who resembles a man as little as possible; a house that preserves of a house exactly what is needed to reveal the metamorphosis; a cone miraculously emerging—as the snake from his slough—from what used to be a mountain. For the modern artist, aesthetic pleasure derives from such a triumph over human matter. That is why he has to drive home the victory by presenting in each case the strangled victim.

It may be thought a simple affair to fight shy of reality, but it is by no means easy. There is no difficulty in painting or saying things which make no sense whatever, which are unintelligible and therefore nothing. One only needs to assemble unconnected words or to draw random lines.* But to construct something that is not a copy of "nature" and yet possesses substance of its own is a feat which presupposes nothing less than genius.

"Reality" constantly waylays the artist to prevent his flight. Much cunning is needed to effect the sublime escape. A reversed Odysseus, he must free himself from his daily Penelope and sail through reefs and rocks to Circe's Faery. When, for a moment, he succeeds in escaping the perpetual ambush, let us not grudge him a gesture of arrogant triumph, a St. George gesture with the dragon prostrate at his feet.

* This was done by the dadaistic hoax. It is interesting to note again (see the above footnote) that the very vagaries and abortive experiments of the new art derive with a certain cogency from its organic principle, thereby giving ample proof that modern art is a unified and meaningful movement.

INVITATION TO UNDERSTANDING

⟨ The works of art that the nineteenth century favored invariably contain a core of "lived" reality which furnishes the substance, as it were, of the aesthetic body. With this material the aesthetic process works, and its working consists in endowing the human nucleus with glamour and dignity. To the majority of people this is the most natural and the only possible setup of a work of art. Art is reflected life, nature seen through a temperament, representation of human destinies, and so on. But the fact is that our young artists, with no less conviction, maintain the opposite. Must the old always have the last word today while tomorrow infallibly the young win out? For one thing, let us not rant and rave. *"Dove si grida,"* Leonardo da Vinci warns us, *"no é vera scienza." "Neque lugere neque indignari sed intelligere,"* recommends Spinoza. Our firmest convictions are apt to be the most suspect, they mark our limits and our bonds. Life is a petty thing unless it is moved by the indomitable urge to extend its boundaries. Only in proportion as we are desirous of living more do we really live. Obstinately to insist on carrying on within the same familiar horizon betrays weakness and a decline of vital energies. Our horizon is a biological line, a living part of our organism. In times of fullness of life it expands, elastically moving in unison almost with our breathing. When the horizon stiffens it is because it has become fossilized and we are growing old.

It is less obvious than academicians assume that a

work of art must consist of human stuff which the Muses comb and groom. Art cannot be reduced to cosmetics. Perception of "lived" reality and perception of artistic form, as I have said before, are essentially incompatible because they call for a different adjustment of our perceptive apparatus. An art that requires such a double seeing is a squinting art. The nineteenth century was remarkably cross-eyed. That is why its products, far from representing a normal type of art, may be said to mark a maximum aberration in the history of taste. All great periods of art have been careful not to let the work revolve about human contents. The imperative of unmitigated realism that dominated the artistic sensibility of the last century must be put down as a freak in aesthetic evolution. It thus appears that the new inspiration, extravagant though it seems, is merely returning, at least in one point, to the royal road of art. For this road is called "will to style." But to stylize means to deform reality, to derealize; style involves dehumanization. And vice versa, there is no other means of stylizing except by dehumanizing. Whereas realism, exhorting the artist faithfully to follow reality, exhorts him to abandon style. A Zurbarán enthusiast, groping for the suggestive word, will declare that the works of this painter have "character." And character and not style is distinctive of the works of Lucas and Sorolla, of Dickens and Galdós. The eighteenth century, on the other hand, which had so little character was a past master of style.

❮ The young set has declared taboo any infiltration of human contents into art. Now, human contents, the component elements of our daily world, form a hierarchy of three ranks. There is first the realm of persons, second that of living beings, lastly there are the inorganic things. The veto of modern art is more or less apodictic according to the rank the respective object holds in this hierarchy. The first stratum, as it is most human, is most carefully avoided.

This is clearly discernible in music and in poetry. From Beethoven to Wagner music was primarily concerned with expressing personal feelings. The composer erected great structures of sound in which to accommodate his autobiography. Art was, more or less, confession. There existed no way of aesthetic enjoyment except by contagion. "In music," Nietzsche declared, "the passions enjoy themselves." Wagner poured into *Tristan and Isolde* his adultery with Mathilde Wesendonck, and if we want to enjoy this work we must, for a few hours, turn vaguely adulterous ourselves. That darkly stirring music makes us weep and tremble and melt away voluptuously. From Beethoven to Wagner all music is melodrama.

And that is unfair, a young artist would say. It means taking advantage of a noble weakness inherent in man which exposes him to infection from his neighbor's joys and sorrows. Such an infection is no mental phenomenon; it works like a reflex in the same way as the grating of a knife upon glass sets the teeth on edge. It is an automatic effect, nothing else. We must distinguish between delight and titillation. Romanticism hunts with a decoy, it tampers with the bird's fervor in order to riddle him with the pellets of sounds. Art must not proceed by psychic contagion, for psychic contagion is an unconscious phenomenon, and art ought to be full clarity, high noon of the intellect. Tears and laughter are, aesthetically, frauds. The gesture of beauty never passes beyond smiles, melancholy or delighted. If it can do without them, better still. *"Toute maîtrise jette le froid"* (Mallarmé).

There is, to my mind, a good deal of truth in the young artist's verdict. Aesthetic pleasure must be a seeing pleasure. For pleasures may be blind or seeing. The drunken man's happiness is blind. Like everything in the world it has a cause, the alcohol; but it has no motive. A man who has won at sweepstakes is happy too, but in a different manner; he is happy "about" something. The drunken man's merriment is hermetically enclosed in itself, he does not know why he is happy. Whereas the joy of the winner consists precisely in his being conscious of a definite fact that motivates and justifies his contentment. He is glad because he is aware of an object that is in itself gladdening. His is a happiness with eyes and which feeds on its motive, flowing, as it were, from the object to the subject.*

* Causation and motivation are two completely different relations. The causes of our states of consciousness are not present in

Any phenomenon that aspires to being mental and not mechanical must bear this luminous character of intelligibility, of motivation. But the pleasure aroused by romantic art has hardly any connection with its content. What has the beauty of music—something obviously located without and beyond myself in the realm of sound—what has the beauty of music to do with that melting mood it may produce in me? Is not this a thorough confusion? Instead of delighting in the artistic object people delight in their own emotions, the work being only the cause and the alcohol of their pleasure. And such a *quid pro quo* is bound to happen whenever art is made to consist essentially in an exposition of "lived" realities. "Lived" realities are too overpowering not to evoke a sympathy which prevents us from perceiving them in their objective purity.

Seeing requires distance. Each art operates a magic lantern that removes and transfigures its objects. On its screen they stand aloof, inmates of an inaccessible world, in an absolute distance. When this derealization is lacking, an awkward perplexity arises: we do not know whether to "live" the things or to observe them.

Madame Tussaud's comes to mind and the peculiar uneasiness aroused by dummies. The origin of this uneasiness lies in the provoking ambiguity with which wax figures defeat any attempt at adopting a clear and consistent attitude toward them. Treat them as living

these states; science must ascertain them. But the motive of a feeling, of a volition, of a belief forms part of the act itself. Motivation is a conscious relation.

beings, and they will sniggeringly reveal their waxen secret. Take them for dolls, and they seem to breathe in irritated protest. They will not be reduced to mere objects. Looking at them we suddenly feel a misgiving: should it not be they who are looking at us? Till in the end we are sick and tired of those hired corpses. Wax figures are melodrama at its purest.

The new sensibility, it seems to me, is dominated by a distaste for human elements in art very similar to the feelings cultured people have always experienced at Madame Tussaud's, while the mob has always been delighted by that gruesome waxen hoax. In passing we may here ask ourselves a few impertinent questions which we have no intention to answer now. What is behind this disgust at seeing art mixed up with life? Could it be disgust for the human sphere as such, for reality, for life? Or is it rather the opposite: respect for life and unwillingness to confuse it with art, so inferior a thing as art? But what do we mean by calling art an inferior function—divine art, glory of civilization, *fine fleur* of culture, and so forth? As we were saying, these questions are impertinent; let us dismiss them.

In Wagner, melodrama comes to a peak. Now, an artistic form, on reaching its maximum, is likely to topple over into its opposite. And thus we find that in Wagner the human voice has already ceased to be the protagonist and is drowned in the cosmic din of the orchestra. However, a more radical change was to follow. Music had to be relieved of private sentiments and purified in an exemplary objectification. This was the deed of Debussy. Owing to him, it has become possible to listen to music serenely, without swoons and tears. All the various developments in the art of music during these last decades move on the ground of the new ultra-worldly world conquered by the genius of Debussy. So decisive is this conversion of the subjective attitude into the objective that any subsequent differentiations appear comparatively negligible.* Debussy dehumanized music, that is why he marks a new era in the art of music.

The same happened in poetry. Poetry had to be disencumbered. Laden with human matter it was dragging along, skirting the ground and bumping into trees and house tops like a deflated balloon. Here Mallarmé was the liberator who restored to the lyrical poem its ethereal quality and ascending power. Perhaps he did not reach the goal himself. Yet it was he who gave the decisive order: shoot ballast.

For what was the theme of poetry in the romantic century? The poet informed us prettily of his private upper-middle-class emotions, his major and minor sorrows, his yearnings, his religious or political preoccupations, and, in case he was English, his reveries behind his pipe. In one way or another, his ambition was to enhance his daily existence. Thanks to personal genius, a halo of finer substance might occasionally surround the human core of the poem—as for instance

* A more detailed analysis of Debussy's significance with respect to romantic music may be found in the author's above quoted essay "Musicalia."

in Baudelaire. But this splendor was a by-product. All the poet wished was to be human.

"And that seems objectionable to a young man?" somebody who has ceased to be one asks with suppressed indignation. "What does he want the poet to be? A bird, an ichthyosaurus, a dodecahedron?"

I can't say. However, I believe that the young poet when writing poetry simply wishes to be a poet. We shall yet see that all new art (like new science, new politics—new life, in sum) abhors nothing so much as blurred borderlines. To insist on neat distinctions is a symptom of mental honesty. Life is one thing, art is another—thus the young set think or at least feel—let us keep the two apart. The poet begins where the man ends. The man's lot is to live his human life, the poet's to invent what is nonexistent. Herein lies the justification of the poetical profession. The poet aggrandizes the world by adding to reality, which is there by itself, the continents of his imagination. Author derives from *auctor*, he who augments. It was the title Rome bestowed upon her generals when they had conquered new territory for the City.

Mallarmé was the first poet in the nineteenth century who wanted to be nothing but a poet. He "eschewed"—as he said himself—"the materials offered by nature" and composed small lyrical objects distinct from the human fauna and flora. This poetry need not be "felt." As it contains nothing human, it contains no cue for emotion either. When a woman is mentioned it is "the woman no one"; when an hour strikes it is "the hour not marked on dials." Proceeding by negatives, Mallarmé's verse muffles all vital resonance and presents us with figures so extramundane that merely looking at them is delight. Among such creatures, what business has the poor face of the man who officiates as poet? None but to disappear, to vanish and to become a pure nameless voice breathing into the air the words—those true protagonists of the lyrical pursuit. This pure and nameless voice, the mere acoustic carrier of the verse, is the voice of the poet who has learned to extricate himself from the surrounding man.

Wherever we look we see the same thing: flight from the human person. The methods of dehumanization are many. Those employed today may differ vastly from Mallarmé's; in fact, I am well aware that his pages are still reached by romantic palpitations. Yet just as modern music belongs to a historical unity that begins with Debussy, all new poetry moves in the direction in which Mallarmé pointed. The landmarks of these two names seem to me essential for charting the main line of the new style above the indentations produced by individual inspirations.

It will not be easy to interest a person under thirty in a book that under the pretext of art reports on the doings of some men and women. To him, such a thing smacks of sociology or psychology. He would accept it gladly if issues were not confused and those facts were told him in sociological and psychological terms. But art means something else to him.

Poetry has become the higher algebra of metaphors.

❰ The metaphor is perhaps one of man's most fruitful potentialities. Its efficacy verges on magic, and it seems a tool for creation which God forgot inside one of His creatures when He made him.

All our other faculties keep us within the realm of the real, of what is already there. The most we can do is to combine things or to break them up. The metaphor alone furnishes an escape; between the real things, it lets emerge imaginary reefs, a crop of floating islands.

A strange thing, indeed, the existence in man of this mental activity which substitutes one thing for another—from an urge not so much to get at the first as to get rid of the second. The metaphor disposes of an object by having it masquerade as something else. Such a procedure would make no sense if we did not discern beneath it an instinctive avoidance of certain realities.*

In his search for the origin of the metaphor a psychologist recently discovered to his surprise that one of its roots lies in the spirit of the taboo.† There was an age when fear formed the strongest incentive of man, an age ruled by cosmic terror. At that time a compulsion was felt to keep clear of certain realities which, on the other hand, could not be entirely avoided. The animal that was most frequent in the region and on which peo-

* More about metaphors may be found in the author's essay "Las dos grandes metáphoras" in *El Espectador* (Madrid, 1925), vol. IV, 153.
† Cf. Heinz Werner, *Die Ursprünge der Metapher*. Leipzig: Engelmann, 1919.

ple depended for food acquired the prestige of something sacred. Such a sanctification implied the idea that a person must not touch that animal with his hands. What then does the Indian Lilloeth do so that he can eat? He squats and folds his hands under his behind. This way he can eat, for hands folded under him are metaphorically feet. Here we have a trope in the form of action, a primordial metaphor preceding verbal imagery and prompted by a desire to get around a reality.

Since to primitive man a word is somehow identical with the thing it stands for, he finds it impossible to name the awful object on which a taboo has fallen. Such an object has to be alluded to by a word denoting something else and thus appears in speech vicariously and surreptitiously. When a Polynesian, who must not call by name anything belonging to the king, sees the torches lighted in the royal hut he will say: "The lightning shines in the clouds of heaven." Here again we have metaphorical elusion.

Once it is obtained in this tabooistic form, the instrument of metaphoric expression can be employed for many diverse purposes. The one predominant in poetry has aimed at exalting the real object. Similes have been used for decorative purposes, to embellish and to throw into relief beloved reality. It would be interesting to find out whether in the new artistic inspiration, where they fulfill a substantive and not a merely decorative function, images have not acquired a curious derogatory quality and, instead of ennobling and enhancing, be-

little and disparage poor reality. I remember reading a
book of modern poetry in which a flash of lightning
was compared to a carpenter's rule and the leafless trees
of winter to brooms sweeping the sky. The weapon of
poetry turns against natural things and wounds or
murders them.

SURREALISM AND INFRAREALISM

⟨ But the metaphor, though the most radical instrument of dehumanization, is certainly not the only one.
There are many of varying scope.

The simplest may be described as a change of perspective. From the standpoint of ordinary human life
things appear in a natural order, a definite hierarchy.
Some seem very important, some less so, and some altogether negligible. To satisfy the desire for dehumanization one need not alter the inherent nature of things. It
is enough to upset the value pattern and to produce an
art in which the small events of life appear in the fore-
ground with monumental dimensions.

Here we have the connecting link between two seemingly very different manners of modern art, the surreal-
ism of metaphors and what may be called infrarealism.
Both satisfy the urge to escape and elude reality. Instead of soaring to poetical heights, art may dive beneath the level marked by the natural perspective.
How it is possible to overcome realism by merely putting too fine a point on it and discovering, lens in hand,

the micro-structure of life can be observed in Proust, Ramón Gómez de la Serna, Joyce.

Ramón can compose an entire book on bosoms—somebody has called him a new Columbus discovering hemispheres—or on the circus, or on the dawn, or on the Rastro and the Puerta del Sol. The procedure simply consists in letting the outskirts of attention, that which ordinarily escapes notice, perform the main part in life's drama. Giraudoux, Morand, etc., employ (in their several ways) the same aesthetic equipment.

That explains Giraudoux's and Morand's enthusiasm for Proust, as it explains in general the admiration shown by the younger set for a writer so thoroughly of another time. The essential trait Proust's amplitudinous novel may have in common with the new sensibility is this change of perspective: contempt for the old monumental forms of the soul and an unhuman attention to the micro-structure of sentiments, social relations, characters.

INVERSION

(In establishing itself in its own right, the metaphor assumes a more or less leading part in the poetical pursuit. This implies that the aesthetic intention has veered round and now points in the opposite direction. Before, reality was overlaid with metaphors by way of ornament; now the tendency is to eliminate the extrapoetical, or real, prop and to "realize" the metaphor, to make it the *res poetica*. This inversion of the aesthetic process is not restricted to the use made of metaphors. It obtains in all artistic means and orders, to the point of determining—in the form of a tendency*—the physiognomy of all contemporary art.

The relation between our mind and things consists in that we think the things, that we form ideas about them. We possess of reality, strictly speaking, nothing but the ideas we have succeeded in forming about it. These ideas are like a belvedere from which we behold the world. Each new idea, as Goethe put it, is like a newly developed organ. By means of ideas we see the world, but in a natural attitude of the mind we do not see the ideas—the same as the eye in seeing does not see itself. In other words, thinking is the endeavor to capture reality by means of ideas; the spontaneous movement of the mind goes from concepts to the world.

But an absolute distance always separates the idea from the thing. The real thing always overflows the concept that is supposed to hold it. An object is more and other than what is implied in the idea of it. The idea remains a bare pattern, a sort of scaffold with which we try to get at reality. Yet a tendency resident in human nature prompts us to assume that reality is what we think of it and thus to confound reality and idea by taking in good faith the latter for the thing itself. Our yearning for reality leads us to an ingenuous idealiza-

* It would be tedious to warn at the foot of each page that each of the features here pointed out as essential to modern art must be understood as existing in the form of a predominant propensity, not of an absolute property.

tion of reality. Such is the innate predisposition of man.

If we now invert the natural direction of this process; if, turning our back on alleged reality, we take the ideas for what they are—mere subjective patterns—and make them live as such, lean and angular, but pure and transparent; in short, if we deliberately propose to "realize" our ideas—then we have dehumanized and, as it were, derealized them. For ideas are really unreal. To regard them as reality is an idealization, a candid falsification. On the other hand, making them live in their very unreality is—let us express it this way—realizing the unreal as such. In this way we do not move from the mind to the world. On the contrary, we give three-dimensional being to mere patterns, we objectify the subjective, we "worldify" the immanent.

A traditional painter painting a portrait claims to have got hold of the real person when, in truth and at best, he has set down on the canvas a schematic selection, arbitrarily decided on by his mind, from the innumerable traits that make a living person. What if the painter changed his mind and decided to paint not the real person but his own idea, his pattern, of the person? Indeed, in that case the portrait would be the truth and nothing but the truth, and failure would no longer be inevitable. In foregoing to emulate reality the painting becomes what it authentically is: an image, an unreality.

Expressionism, cubism, etc., are—in varying degree—attempts at executing this decision. From painting things, the painter has turned to painting ideas. He shuts his eyes to the outer world and concentrates upon the subjective images in his own mind.

Notwithstanding its crudeness and the hopeless vulgarity of its subject, Pirandello's drama *Six Personages in Search of an Author* is, from the point of view of an aesthetic theory of the drama, perhaps one of the most interesting recent plays. It supplies an excellent example of this inversion of the artistic attitude which I am trying to describe. The traditional playwright expects us to take his personages for persons and their gestures for the indications of a "human" drama. Whereas here our interest is aroused by some personages as such—that is, as ideas or pure patterns.

Pirandello's drama is, I dare say, the first "drama of ideas" proper. All the others that bore this name were not dramas of ideas, but dramas among pseudo persons symbolizing ideas. In Pirandello's work, the sad lot of each of the six personages is a mere pretext and remains shadowy. Instead, we witness the real drama of some ideas as such, some subjective phantoms gesticulating in an author's mind. The artist's intent to dehumanize is unmistakable, and conclusive proof is given of the possibility of executing it. At the same time, this work provides a model instance for the difficulty of the average public to accommodate their vision to such an inverted perspective. They are looking for the human drama which the artist insists on presenting in an offhand, elusive, mocking manner putting in its place— that is, in the first place—the theatrical fiction itself. Average theater-goers resent that he will not deceive them, and refuse to be amused by that delightful fraud of art—all the more exquisite the more frankly it reveals its fraudulent nature.

ICONOCLASM

❨ It is not an exaggeration to assert that modern paintings and sculptures betray a real loathing of living forms or forms of living beings. The phenomenon becomes particularly clear if the art of these last years is compared with that sublime hour when painting and sculpture emerge from Gothic discipline as from a nightmare and bring forth the abundant, world-wide harvest of the Renaissance. Brush and chisel delight in rendering the exuberant forms of the model—man, animal, or plant. All bodies are welcome, if only life with its dynamic power is felt to throb in them. And from paintings and sculptures organic form flows over into ornament. It is the epoch of the cornucopias whose torrential fecundity threatens to flood all space with round, ripe fruits.

Why is it that the round and soft forms of living bodies are repulsive to the present-day artist? Why does he replace them with geometric patterns? For with all the blunders and all the sleights of hand of cubism, the fact remains that for some time we have been well pleased with a language of pure Euclidean patterns.

The phenomenon becomes more complex when we remember that crazes of this kind have periodically recurred in history. Even in the evolution of prehistoric art we observe that artistic sensibility begins with seeking the living form and then drops it, as though affrighted and nauseated, and resorts to abstract signs, the last residues of cosmic or animal forms. The serpent is stylized into the meander, the sun into the swastica. At times, this disgust at living forms flares up and produces public conflicts. The revolt against the images of Oriental Christianism, the Semitic law forbidding representation of animals—an attitude opposite to the instinct of those people who decorated the cave of Altamira—doubtless originate not only in a religious feeling but also in an aesthetic sensibility whose subsequent influence on Byzantine art is clearly discernible.

A thorough investigation of such eruptions of iconoclasm in religion and art would be of high interest. Modern art is obviously actuated by one of these curious iconoclastic urges. It might have chosen for its motto the commandment of Porphyrius which, in its Manichaean adaptation, was so violently opposed by St. Augustine: *Omne corpus fugiendum est*—where *corpus*, to be sure, must be understood as "living body." A curious contrast indeed with Greek culture which at its height was so deeply in love with living forms.

NEGATIVE INFLUENCE OF THE PAST

❨ This essay, as I have said before, confines itself to delineating the new art by means of some of its distinguishing features. However, it is prompted by a curiosity of wider scope which these pages do not venture to satisfy but only wish to arouse in the reader; whereupon we shall leave him to his own meditations.

Elsewhere* I have pointed out that it is in art and pure science, precisely because they are the freest activities and least dependent on social conditions, that the first signs of any changes of collective sensibility become noticeable. A fundamental revision of man's attitude towards life is apt to find its first expression in artistic creation and scientific theory. The fine texture of both these matters renders them susceptible to the slightest breeze of the spiritual trade-winds. As in the country, opening the window of a morning, we examine the smoke rising from the chimney-stacks in order to determine the wind that will rule the day, thus we can, with a similar meteorologic purpose, study the art and science of the young generation.

The first step has been to describe the new phenomenon. Only now that this is done can we proceed to ask of which new general style of life modern art is the symptom and the harbinger. The answer requires an analysis of the causes that have effected this strange about-face in art. Why this desire to dehumanize? Why this disgust at living forms? Like all historical phenomena this too will have grown from a multitude of entangled roots which only a fine flair is capable of detecting. An investigation of this kind would be too serious a task to be attacked here. However, what other

* Cf. The author's book *The Modern Theme* (The C. W. Daniel Company, London: 1931), p. 26.

causes may exist, there is one which, though perhaps not decisive, is certainly very clear.

We can hardly put too much stress on the influence which at all times the past of art exerts on the future of art. In the mind of the artist a sort of chemical reaction is set going by the clash between his individual sensibility and already existing art. He does not find himself all alone with the world before him; in his relations with the world there always intervenes, like an interpreter, the artistic tradition. What will the reaction of creative originality upon the beauty of previous works be like? It may be positive or negative. Either the artist is in conformity with the past and regards it as his heritage which he feels called upon to perfect; or he discovers that he has a spontaneous indefinable aversion against established and generally acclaimed art. And as in the first case he will be pleased to settle down in the customary forms and repeat some of their sacred patterns, thus he will, in the second, not only deviate from established tradition but be equally pleased to give to his work an explicit note of protest against the time-honored norms.

The latter is apt to be overlooked when one speaks of the influence of the past on the present. That a work of a certain period may be modeled after works of another previous period has always been easily recognized. But to notice the negative influence of the past and to realize that a new style has not infrequently grown out of a conscious and relished antagonism to traditional styles seems to require somewhat of an effort.

As it is, the development of art from Romanticism to

this day cannot be understood unless this negative mood of mocking aggressiveness is taken into account as a factor of aesthetic pleasure. Baudelaire praises the black Venus precisely because the classical is white. From then on the successive styles contain an ever increasing dose of derision and disparagement until in our day the new art consists almost exclusively of protests against the old. The reason is not far to seek. When an art looks back on many centuries of continuous evolution without major hiatuses or historical catastrophes its products keep on accumulating, and the weight of tradition increasingly encumbers the inspiration of the hour. Or to put it differently, an ever growing mass of traditional styles hampers the direct and original communication between the nascent artist and the world around him. In this case one of two things may happen. Either tradition stifles all creative power—as in Egypt, Byzantium, and the Orient in general—or the effect of the past on the present changes its sign and a long epoch appears in which the new art, step by step, breaks free of the old which threatened to smother it. The latter is typical of Europe whose futuristic instinct, predominant throughout its history, stands in marked contrast to the irremediable traditionalism of the Orient.

A good deal of what I have called dehumanization and disgust for living forms is inspired by just such an aversion against the traditional interpretation of realities. The vigor of the assault stands in inverse proportion to the distance. Keenest contempt is felt for nineteenth century procedures although they contain already a noticeable dose of opposition to older styles. On the other hand, the new sensibility exhibits a somewhat suspicious enthusiasm for art that is most remote in time and space, for prehistoric or savage primitivism. In point of fact, what attracts the modern artist in those primordial works is not so much their artistic quality as their candor; that is, the absence of tradition.

If we now briefly consider the question: What type of life reveals itself in this attack on past art? we come upon a strange and stirring fact. To assail all previous art, what else can it mean than to turn against Art itself? For what is art, concretely speaking, if not such art as has been made up to now?

Should that enthusiasm for pure art be but a mask which conceals surfeit with art and hatred of it? But, how can such a thing come about? Hatred of art is unlikely to develop as an isolated phenomenon; it goes hand in hand with hatred of science, hatred of State, hatred, in sum, of civilization as a whole. Is it conceivable that modern Western man bears a rankling grudge against his own historical essence? Does he feel something akin to the *odium professionis* of medieval monks —that aversion, after long years of monastic discipline, against the very rules that had shaped their lives?*

* It would be interesting to analyze the psychological mechanisms through which yesterday's art negatively affects the art of today. One is obvious: ennui. Mere repetition of a style has a blunting and tiring effect. In his *Principles of Art History; the Problem of the Development of Style in Later Art* (London: Bell, 1932) Heinrich Wölfflin mentions the power of boredom which

This is the moment prudently to lay down one's pen and let a flock of questions take off on their winged course.

DOOMED TO IRONY

❨ When we discovered that the new style taken in its most general aspect is characterized by a tendency to eliminate all that is human and to preserve only the purely artistic elements, this seemed to betray a great enthusiasm for art. But when we then walked around the phenomenon and looked at it from another angle we came upon an unexpected grimace of surfeit or disdain. The contradiction is obvious and must be strongly stressed. It definitely indicates that modern art is of an ambiguous nature which, as a matter of fact, does not surprise us; for ambiguous have been all important issues of these current years. A brief analysis of the political development in Europe would reveal the same intrinsic ambiguity.

However, in the case of art, the contradiction between love and hatred for one and the same thing will appear somewhat mitigated after a closer inspection of present-day artistic production.

---

has ever again mobilized art and compelled it to invent new forms. And the same applies to literature, only more so. Cicero still said *"latine loqui"* for "speaking Latin"; but in the fifth century Apollinaris Sidonius resorted to *"latialiter insusurrare."* For too many centuries the same had been said with the same words.

The first consequence of the retreat of art upon itself is a ban on all pathos. Art laden with "humanity" had become as weighty as life itself. It was an extremely serious affair, almost sacred. At times—in Schopenhauer and Wagner—it aspired to nothing less than to save mankind. Whereas the modern inspiration—and this is a strange fact indeed—is invariably waggish. The waggery may be more or less refined, it may run the whole gamut from open clownery to a slight ironical twinkle, but it is always there. And it is not that the content of the work is comical—that would mean a relapse into a mode or species of the "human" style—but that, whatever the content, the art itself is jesting. To look for fiction as fiction—which, we have said, modern art does—is a proposition that cannot be executed except with one's tongue in one's cheek. Art is appreciated precisely because it is recognized as a farce. It is this trait more than any other that makes the works of the young so incomprehensible to serious people of less progressive taste. To them modern painting and music are sheer "farce"—in the bad sense of the word—and they will not be convinced that to be a farce may be precisely the mission and the virtue of art. A "farce" in the bad sense of the word it would be if the modern artist pretended to equal status with the "serious" artists of the past, and a cubist painting expected to be extolled as solemnly and all but religiously as a statue by Michelangelo. But all he does is to invite us to look at a piece of art that is a joke and that essentially makes fun of itself. For this is what the facetious quality of the modern inspiration comes down to. Instead of deriding other persons or things—without a victim no comedy—the new art ridicules art itself.

And why be scandalized at this? Art has never shown more clearly its magic gift than in this flout at itself. Thanks to this suicidal gesture art continues to be art, its self-negation miraculously bringing about its preservation and triumph.

I much doubt that any young person of our time can be impressed by a poem, a painting, or a piece of music that is not flavored with a dash of irony.

Nor is this ironical reflection of art upon itself entirely new as an idea and a theory. In the beginning of the last century a group of German romanticists, under the leadership of the two brothers Schlegel, pronounced irony the foremost aesthetic category, their reasons being much the same as those of our young artists. Art has no right to exist if, content to reproduce reality, it uselessly duplicates it. Its mission is to conjure up imaginary worlds. That can be done only if the artist repudiates reality and by this act places himself above it. Being an artist means ceasing to take seriously that very serious person we are when we are not an artist.

This inevitable dash of irony, it is true, imparts to modern art a monotony which must exasperate patience herself. But be that as it may, the contradiction between surfeit and enthusiasm now appears resolved. The first is aroused by art as a serious affair, the second is felt for art that triumphs as a farce, laughing off everything, itself included—much as in a system of mirrors which indefinitely reflect one another no shape is ultimate, all are eventually ridiculed and revealed as pure images.

ART A THING
OF NO CONSEQUENCE

(All we have ascertained so far will now appear integrated in the most acute, serious, and deep-seated symptom shown by modern art—a strange feature, indeed, and which requires cautious consideration. What I mean is difficult to express for several reasons, but mainly because it is a matter of accurate formulation.

To the young generation art is a thing of no consequence. —The sentence is no sooner written than it frightens me since I am well aware of all the different connotations it implies. It is not that to any random person of our day art seems less important than it seemed to previous generations, but that the artist himself regards his art as a thing of no consequence. But then again this does not accurately describe the situation. I do not mean to say that the artist makes light of his work and his profession; but they interest him precisely because they are of no transcendent importance. For a real understanding of what is happening let us compare the role art is playing today with the role it used to play thirty years ago and in general throughout the last century. Poetry and music then were activities of an enormous caliber. In view of the downfall of religion and the inevitable relativism of science, art was expected to take upon itself nothing less than the salvation of mankind. Art was important for two reasons: on account of its subjects which dealt with the profoundest problems of humanity, and on account of its own significance as a human pursuit from which the species derived its justification and dignity. It was a remarkable sight, the solemn air with which the great poet or the musical genius appeared before the masses—the air of a prophet and founder of religion, the majestic pose of a statesman responsible for the state of the world.

A present-day artist would be thunderstruck, I suspect, if he were trusted with so enormous a mission and, in consequence, compelled to deal in his work with matters of such scope. To his mind, the kingdom of art commences where the air feels lighter and things, free from formal fetters, begin to cut whimsical capers. In this universal pirouetting he recognizes the best warrant for the existence of the Muses. Were art to redeem man, it could do so only by saving him from the seriousness of life and restoring him to an unexpected boyishness. The symbol of art is seen again in the magic flute of the Great God Pan which makes the young goats frisk at the edge of the grove.

All modern art begins to appear comprehensible and in a way great when it is interpreted as an attempt to instill youthfulness into an ancient world. Other styles must be interpreted in connection with dramatic social or political movements, or with profound religious and philosophical currents. The new style only asks to be linked to the triumph of sports and games. It is of the same kind and origin with them.

In these last few years we have seen almost all caravels of seriousness founder in the tidal wave of sports that floods the newspaper pages. Editorials threaten to be sucked into the abyss of their headlines, and across the surface victoriously sail the yachts of the regattas. Cult of the body is an infallible symptom of a leaning toward youth, for only the young body is lithe and beautiful. Whereas cult of the mind betrays the resolve to accept old age, for the mind reaches plenitude only when the body begins to decline. The triumph of sport marks the victory of the values of youth over the values of age. Note in this context the success of the motion picture, a preeminently corporeal art.

In my generation the manners of old age still enjoyed great prestige. So anxious were boys to cease being boys that they imitated the stoop of their elders. Today children want to prolong their childhood, and boys and girls their youth. No doubt, Europe is entering upon an era of youthfulness.

Nor need this fact surprise us. History moves in long biological rhythms whose chief phases necessarily are brought about not by secondary causes relating to details but by fundamental factors and primary forces of a cosmic nature. It is inconceivable that the major and, as it were, polar differences inherent in the living organism—sex and age—should not decisively mold the profile of the times. Indeed, it can be easily observed that

history is rhythmically swinging back and forth between these two poles, stressing the masculine qualities
in some epochs and the feminine in others, or exalting
now a youthful deportment and then again maturity
and old age.

The aspect European existence is taking on in all
orders of life points to a time of masculinity and youthfulness. For a while women and old people will have to
cede the rule over life to boys; no wonder that the world
grows increasingly informal.

All peculiarities of modern art can be summed up in
this one feature of its renouncing its importance—a feature which, in its turn, signifies nothing less than that
art has changed its position in the hierarchy of human
activities and interests. These activities and interests
may be represented by a series of concentric circles
whose radii measure the dynamic distances from the
axis of life where the supreme desires are operating. All
human matters—vital and cultural—revolve in their
several orbits about the throbbing heart of the system.
Art which—like science and politics—used to be very
near the axis of enthusiasm, that backbone of our person, has moved toward the outer rings. It has lost none
of its attributes, but it has become a minor issue.

The trend toward pure art betrays not arrogance, as
is often thought, but modesty. Art that has rid itself of
human pathos is a thing without consequence—just art
with no other pretenses.

CONCLUSION

❐ Isis *myrionoma*, Isis of the ten thousand names, the Egyptians called their goddess. And a thing with ten thousand names all reality is, in a way. Its components and its facets are countless. Is it not brazen to attempt a definition of any thing, of the humblest thing, with a few names? A stroke of luck it would be if the attributes here pointed out among an infinite number were in fact the decisive ones. The odds are particularly poor since the object is a nascent reality which just begins its course through space.

Thus chances are that this attempt to analyze modern art is full of errors. Now that I am about to conclude it the place it has been taking up in my mind is filled with the hope that others may tackle these problems more successfully. Among many tongues may be divided the calling of the ten thousand names.

But it would not mean improving upon my errors if one tried to correct them by pointing out this or that particular feature omitted in my analysis. Artists are apt to make this mistake when, speaking of their art, they fail to take the step back that affords an ample view of the facts. There can be no doubt that the best approximation to truth is contrived by a formula that in one unified, harmonious turn encompasses the greatest number of particular facts—like a loom which with one stroke interlaces a thousand threads.

I have been moved exclusively by the delight of trying to understand—and neither by ire nor by enthusiasm. I have sought to ascertain the meaning of the new intents of art and that, of course, presupposes an attitude of preconceived benevolence. But is it possible to approach a subject in another mind and not condemn it to barrenness?

It may be said that the new art has so far produced nothing worth while, and I am inclined to think the same. I have proposed to extract from the work of the young the intention which is the juicy part, and I have disregarded the realization. Who knows what may come out of this budding style? The task it sets itself is enormous; it wants to create from nought. Later, I expect, it will be content with less and achieve more.

But whatever their shortcomings, the young artists have to be granted one point: there is no turning back. All the doubts cast upon the inspiration of those pioneers may be justified, and yet they provide no sufficient reason for condemning them. The objections would have to be supplemented by something positive: a suggestion of another way for art different from dehumanization and yet not coincident with the beaten and worn-out paths.

It is easy to protest that it is always possible to produce art within the bounds of a given tradition. But this comforting phrase is of no use to the artist who, pen or chisel in hand, sits waiting for a concrete inspiration.

NOTES ON THE NOVEL

*P*ublishers complain that novels do not sell well, and it is true that the reading public buys fewer novels while the demand for books of a theoretical character is relatively increasing. This statistical fact, even if there were no more intrinsic reasons, would suffice to make us suspect that something is amiss with the literary genre of the novel. When I hear a friend, particularly if he is a young writer, calmly announce that he is working on a novel I am appalled, and I feel that in his case I should be trembling in my boots. Perhaps I am wrong, but I cannot help scenting behind such an equanimity an alarming dose of incomprehension. To produce a good novel has always been a difficult thing. But while, before, it was enough to have talent the difficulty has now grown immeasurably, for to be a gifted novelist is no longer a guaranty for producing a good novel.

Unawareness of this fact is one component of the aforementioned incomprehension. Anyone who gives a little thought to the conditions of a work of art must admit that a literary genre may wear out. One cannot dismiss the subject by comfortably assuming that artistic creation depends on nothing but the artist's personal power called inspiration or talent—in which case decadence of a genre would be due exclusively to an accidental lack of talents, and the sudden appearance of a man of genius would at any time automatically turn the tide. Better beware of notions like genius and inspiration; they are a sort of magic wand and should be used sparingly by anybody who wants to see things clearly. Imagine a woodsman, the strongest of woodsmen, in the Sahara desert. What good are his bulging muscles and his sharp ax? A woodsman without woods is an abstraction. And the same applies to artists. Talent is but a subjective disposition that is brought to bear upon a certain material. The material is independent of individual gifts; and when it is lacking genius and skill are of no avail.

Just as every animal belongs to a species, every literary work belongs to a genre. (The theory of Benedetto Croce who denies the existence of literary forms in this sense has left no trace in aesthetics.) A literary genre, the same as a zoological species, means a certain stock of possibilities; and since in art only those possibilities count which are different enough not to be considered replicas of one another, the resources of a literary genre are definitely limited. It is erroneous to think of the novel—and I refer to the modern novel in particular— as of an endless field capable of rendering ever new forms. Rather it may be compared to a vast but finite quarry. There exist a definite number of possible themes for the novel. The workmen of the primal hour had no trouble finding new blocks—new characters, new themes. But present-day writers face the fact that only narrow and concealed veins are left them.

With this stock of objective possibilities, which is the genre, the artistic talent works, and when the quarry is worked out talent, however great, can achieve nothing. Whether a genre is altogether done for can, of course, never be decided with mathematical rigor; but it can at times be decided with sufficient practical approximation. At least, that the material is getting scarce may appear frankly evident.

This, I believe, is now happening to the novel. It has become practically impossible to find new subjects. Here we come upon the first cause of the enormous difficulty, an objective not a personal difficulty, of writing an acceptable novel at this advanced stage.

During a certain period novels could thrive on the mere novelty of their subjects which gratuitously added an induced current, as it were, to the value proper of the material. Thus many novels seemed readable which we now think a bore. It is not for nothing that the novel is called "novel." The difficulty of finding new subjects is accompanied by another, perhaps more serious, dilemma. As the store of possible subjects is more and more depleted the sensibility of the reading public becomes subtler and more fastidious. Works that yesterday would still have passed, today are deemed insipid. Not only is the difficulty of finding new subjects steadily growing, but ever "newer" and more extraordinary ones are needed to impress the reader. This is the second cause of the difficulty with which the genre as such is faced in our time.

Proof that the present decline is due to more fundamental causes than a possibly inferior quality of contemporary novels is given by the fact that, as it becomes more difficult to write novels, the famous old or classical ones appear less good. Only a very few have escaped drowning in the reader's boredom.

This development is inevitable and need not dishearten the novelists. On the contrary; for they themselves are bringing it about. Little by little they train their public by sharpening the perception, and refining the taste, of their readers. Each work that is better than a previous one is detrimental to this and all others of the same level. Triumph cannot help being cruel. As the victor wins the battle at the cost of smashing the foe, thus the superior work automatically becomes the undoing of scores of other works that used to be highly thought of.

In short, I believe that the genre of the novel, if it is not yet irretrievably exhausted, has certainly entered its last phase, the scarcity of possible subjects being such that writers must make up for it by the exquisite quality of the other elements that compose the body of a novel.

AUTOPSY

❨ It cannot be denied that to us the great Balzac, save for one or two of his books, makes rather difficult reading. Our perceptive apparatus, used to more distinct and genuine spectacles, detects at once the conventional, artificial and à-peu-près complexion of the world of the *Human Comedy*. Were I asked why I find fault with Balzac I should answer: Because he is a dauber.

What distinguishes the dauber from the good painter? That on the latter's painting the object it represents is there in person, as it were, in the fullness of its being, in self-presence. Whereas the former, instead of presenting the object itself, sets down on his canvas only a few feeble and unessential allusions to it. The longer we look at his work, the clearer it becomes that the object is not there.

This difference between self-presence and mere allusion seems to me decisive in all art but very specially in the novel.

The subject of *Le rouge et le noir* could be told in a few dozen words. What is the difference between such a report and the novel itself? Certainly not the style. The crucial point is that when we say: "Madame Renal falls in love with Julien Sorel" we merely allude to this fact while Stendhal presents it in its immediate and patent reality.

Now, an examination of the evolution of the novel from its beginnings to our day reveals that, from being pure narration which but alludes, the novel has advanced to strict presentation. At first, the narrative as such kept the reader amused through the novelty of the subject. He was as delighted to listen to the hero's adventures as we are to hear what has happened to a person we love. But soon adventures by themselves lose attraction, and what then pleases is not so much the fortunes of the personages as their self-presence. We enjoy seeing those people before us and being admitted to their inner life, understanding them, and living immersed in their world or atmosphere. From being narrative and indirect the novel has become direct and descriptive. The best word would be "presentative." The imperative of the novel is autopsy. No good telling us what a person is, we want to see with our own eyes.

Analyze such ancient novels as have survived in the appreciation of responsible readers, and it will appear that they all use the autoptic method. Above all *Don Quixote*. Cervantes fills all our senses with the genuine presence of his personages. We listen to their true conversations, we see their actual movements. Stendhal's greatness derives from the same cause.

NO DEFINITIONS

(We want to see the life of the figures in a novel, not to be told it. Any reference, allusion, narration only emphasizes the absence of what it alludes to. Things that are there need not be related.

Hence one of the major errors a novelist can commit consists in attempting to define his personages.

It is the task of science to work out definitions. All scientific endeavor lastly consists in the systematic effort to leave behind the object and to arrive at its definition. Now, a definition is nothing if not a series of concepts, and a concept is nothing else than a mental allusion to an object. The concept "red" contains no red; it is merely a movement of the mind toward the color of this name, a sign pointing in the direction of this color.

It has been said by Wundt, if I remember right, that the most primitive form of a concept is the pointing gesture of the index finger. An infant still tries to take hold of any object that enters his field of vision because his undeveloped sense of perspective prevents him from judging distances. After many failures he gives up and contents himself with indicating the object with his outstretched hand—a symbolic capture. The true function of concepts is to point or to indicate. Science is concerned not with things but with the system of signs it can substitute for things.

Art, on the other hand, urged by a magnificent impulse to see, turns from the conventional signs to the things themselves. There is a good deal of truth in Fiedler's assertion that the aim of painting is to furnish a fuller and completer view of things than can be obtained in the ordinary intercourse with them.

The same, I believe, applies to the novel. In its beginnings the plot may have seemed to form its most important part. Later it appeared that what really matters is not the story which is told but that the story, whatever it might be, should be told well. From our present-day standpoint the primitive novel seems more narrative than the modern. However, this impression may have to be revised. Perhaps a primitive reader resembled a child in that he was capable of seeing in a few lines, in a bare pattern the integral object with vigorous presence. (Primitive sculpture and certain new psychological discoveries of great importance corroborate this belief.) In that case the novel would, strictly speaking, not have changed; its present descriptive, or rather presentative, form would merely be the means that had to be used in order to produce in a limp sensibility the same effect which in more springy souls had been obtained by narration.

When I read in a novel "John was peevish" it is as though the writer invited me to visualize, on the strength of his definition, John's peevishness in my own imagination. That is to say, he expects me to be the novelist. What is required, I should think, is exactly the opposite: that he furnish the visible facts so that I obligingly discover and define John to be peevish. A novelist must proceed in the same way as the impressionistic painters who set down on the canvas such elements as the spectator needs for seeing an apple, and leave it to him to give to this material the finishing touches. Hence the fresh taste of all impressionistic painting. We seem to see the objects of the picture in a perpetual *status nascendi*. In the career of every thing there are two moments of supreme drama: birth and death—*status nascens* and *status evanescens*. Nonimpressionistic painting, superior though it may be in other respects, suffers from one shortcoming: that it presents its objects altogether finished, mummified and, as it were, past. That actuality, that existence in the present tense, which things possess in impressionistic pictures is irremediably missing.

❡ Hence the present-day novel must be the opposite of a story. A story relates events; the accent is on action. The fresh mind of a child is interested in adventure as such—perhaps, as we were saying, because the child sees in palpable presence what our imagination is too weak to visualize. Adventures do not interest us; or at least, they interest only the child that, as a somewhat barbarous residue, we all carry inside. The rest of our person is not susceptible to the mechanical thrill of, say, a dime novel; and so we feel, after having finished reading such products, a bad taste in our mouth as though we had indulged in a base pleasure. It is not easy nowadays to invent adventures capable of stirring the superior portion of our sensibility.

Action thus becomes a mere pretext—the string, as it were, that makes the beads into a necklace. Why that string cannot be dispensed with, will appear later on. At this point I wish to draw attention to the fact that when a novel bores us it is not, as an insufficient analysis may lead us to believe, because "its subject is uninteresting." If that were so we might as well declare the entire species dead and buried. For the impossibility of inventing new "interesting subjects" is all too patent.

No, when we are fascinated by a novel it is not because of its subject, not because we are curious to know what happened to Mr. So-and-so. The subject of any novel can be told in a few words and in this form holds no interest. A summary narration is not to our taste;

we want the novelist to linger and to grant us good long looks at his personages, their being, and their environment till we have had our fill and feel that they are close friends whom we know thoroughly in all the wealth of their lives. That is what makes of the novel an essentially slow-moving genre, as either Goethe or Novalis observed. I will go even further and say that today the novel is, and must be, a sluggish form—the very opposite therefore of a story, a "serial," or a thriller.

I have sometimes tried to explain the pleasure—a mild pleasure, to be sure—aroused by certain American films that consist of a long series of episodes. (But the word "episode" is absurd; a work made of episodes would be like a meal composed of side-dishes.) And I found to my great surprise that I felt entertained not by the stupid subject but by the personages themselves. A film in which the detective and the young American girl are attractive may go on indefinitely and never become boring. It does not matter what they do; we simply enjoy watching them. They interest us not because of what they are doing; rather the opposite, what they do interests us because it is they who do it.

Let the reader recall the great novels of former days that have lived up to the high standards of our time, and he will observe that his attention is turned to the personages themselves, not to their adventures. We are fascinated by Don Quixote and Sancho, not by what is happening to them. In principle, a *Don Quixote* as great as the original is conceivable in which the knight and his servant go through entirely different experiences. And the same holds for Julien Sorel or David Copperfield.

FUNCTION AND SUBSTANCE

⟨ Our interest has shifted from the plot to the figures, from actions to persons. Now, this transference—let it be noted parenthetically—finds a counterpart in what has, these last twenty years, been happening in physics and, above all, in philosophy. From Kant to about 1900 we observe a determinate tendency in theoretical thought to eliminate substances and to replace them by functions. In Greece and in the Middle Ages it was believed that *operari sequitur esse*—actions follow, and derive from, being. The nineteenth century may be said to have established the opposite principle: *esse sequitur operari*—the being of a thing is nothing else than the sum total of its actions and functions.

Should we, by any chance, now be again in the process of turning from action to the person, from function to substance? Such a transition would be indicative of an emerging classicism.

But this question deserves more comment, and it invites us to seek further orientation through a comparison of the classical French theater with the indigenous Spanish theater.

❲ Not many things illuminate the finer points of the diversity of French and Spanish destinies so well as the difference of structure between the classical French theater and the indigenous Spanish theater. I do not call the latter classical; for, without detriment to any of its other virtues, the character of classicism must be denied it. The Spanish theater is popular; and nothing in history, as far as I can see, has ever been classical and popular at once. The French tragedy, on the other hand, is an art for aristocrats. Thus it already differs from the Spanish regarding the class of people to which it addresses itself. Furthermore, its aesthetic intention is approximately the opposite of that of our popular playwrights. This must, of course, be understood as referring to both styles in their totality; either may admit of exceptions which are, as always, required to prove the rule.

In French tragedies, action is reduced to a minimum. Not only in the sense of the three unities (we shall yet see how important these are to the novel "that has to be written") but also in so far as the story that is told is cut down to the smallest size. Our theater amasses whatever adventures and changes of fortune it can possibly think of; one feels that the author has to entertain an audience already stirred up by a life of new and perilous experiences. The French tragedian wants to set down on the canvas of a well-known "history," which in itself holds no longer any dramatic interest, three or four significant motives. Mere physical adventures he rather avoids; the events of outer life serve only to present certain inner problems. The author and his audience enjoy not so much the passions and the consequent dramatic entanglements of the personages as the analysis of those passions; whereas in the Spanish theater psychological anatomy of sentiments and characters is infrequent or at least unimportant. Sentiments and characters are taken from without as a whole and used as a springboard from which the drama or adventure takes off for its headlong leap. Anything else would have bored the audience of a Spanish *corral*, an audience of simple souls given to passion rather than to contemplation.

However, psychological analysis is not the last aim of French tragedies; it serves as a vehicle for another purpose which manifestly relates the French theater to Greek and Roman theater. (Seneca's influence on the classical French drama can hardly be overrated.) The aristocratic audience enjoys the exemplary and normative character of the tragic happenings. They go to the theater not to be stirred by Athalie's or Phèdre's anguish but to feel elated by the model deportment of those great-hearted figures. In the last instance, French theater is ethical contemplation, not vital emotion like the Spanish. What it presents is not a series of ethically neutral incidents but an exemplary type of reaction, a repertory of normative attitudes in the supreme crises of life. The personages are heroes, exalted characters, prototypes of magnanimity. There appear on this scene only kings and peers—human beings who, exempt from the common urgencies of life, can freely devote their exuberant energies to purely moral conflicts. Even if we did not know the French society of that time, those tragedies would suggest an audience of people preoccupied with the high forms of seemliness and with their own perfection. The style is measured and of a noble tenor; it admits of neither coarseness, which may be so enlivening, nor utter frenzy. Passion never loses control of itself; proceeding with meticulous correctness of form, it keeps within the bounds of poetical, urbane, and even grammatical laws. French tragic art is the art of not letting fly, of always subjecting word and gesture to the highest regulative norm. In brief, French tragedies reveal that same will to selection and deliberate refinement that has, generation after generation, mellowed French life and French people.

In every order of life, abandonment is characteristic of the popular spirit. Popular religions have always reveled in orgiastic rites, and their excesses have always been opposed by the religious feeling of select minds. Brahmans fight against magic, Confucian mandarins against Taoistic superstition, Catholic councils against mystic ecstasy. Let us sum up these two antagonistic vital attitudes by saying that for the one, the noble and exacting one, ideal life consists in self-control, while to the other, the popular, to live means to surrender to the surge of emotion and to seek unconsciousness and frenzy in passion, orgies, or alcohol.

The Spanish public found something of the second

kind in the fiery plays our poets produced. And this confirms rather unexpectedly the condition of a people of "people" that, in an earlier book,* I have maintained to be discernible throughout the history of Spain. Not selection and measure, but passion and abandonment. No doubt, this thirst for strong brew is not conducive to greatness. I am not now concerned with considering the value of races and styles but with briefly adumbrating two contrary temperaments.

In general, the personalities of the men and women in Spanish plays remain blurred. What is interesting about them is not their characters but that they are seen roving through the wide world, tossed about by the whirlwind of adventure. Disheveled ladies lost in the Sierras, who yesterday appeared in grand attire in the soft light of drawing rooms and tomorrow, masked as Moors, may sail into the port of Constantinople. Sudden infatuations, as though by witchery, of burning hearts without gravity. That was what attracted our forefathers. In a delightful essay, Azorín describes a theatrical performance in the *corral* of an old Spanish village. The chivalrous lover, his life hanging by a thread, uses the most precarious moment to propose to his lady in flashy verse sparkling like torches with a wonderful rhetoric full of baroque flourishes and laden with images through which the entire flora and fauna is moving—that rhetoric which in sculpture engenders the post-Renaissance consoles with their trophies, their

* Cf. the author's book *Invertebrate Spain*. New York: W. W. Norton, 1937.

fruits, their pennants, and their heads of goats and rams. At this moment the dark eyes of one of the spectators, a scholar in his fifties, begin to burn in his waxen face, and with a nervous hand he caresses his grizzled goatee. This paragraph of Azorín's has taught me more about the Spanish theater than all the books I have read.* Inflammable matter the Spanish theater was—that is to say, a thing as distinct as possible from the norm of perfection the French theater aspired to be. Not for the sake of watching noble souls behave exemplarily did the good Castilian go to see the famous play, but to be swept off his feet and to get drunk on the potent draught of the adventures and ordeals of the personages. Over the intricate and varied pattern of the intrigue the poet poured his elaborate volubility—a profusion of glittering metaphors expressed in a vocabulary of darkest shadows alternating with brilliant light, a vocabulary reminiscent of the altar-pieces of that same century. Added to the conflagration of passionate destinies the audience found an imagination all aflame in the fireworks of Lope's and Calderón's quatrains.

The substance of the pleasure contained in our theater is of the same Dionysian kind with the mystic raptures of seventeenth century monks and nuns, those sublime indulgers in ecstasy. Not a grain of contemplation. Contemplation requires a cool head and a certain distance between the object and oneself. When we wish

* Cf. Américo Castro's introduction to the plays of Tirso de Molina, Clásicos Castellanos, Ediciones de la Lectura, Madrid.

to watch a torrent, the first thing to see to is that we are not swept away by it.

Two opposite artistic intentions, we thus find, are operating in these two theaters. In the Castilian drama the stress is on action, on destinies rich in vicissitudes and, at the same time, on the lyrical embellishment of ornate verse. In the French tragedy the essential thing is the personages themselves and their exemplary and paradigmatic nature. That is why Racine's work impresses us as cold, a monochrome. We feel ushered into a garden where some statues converse and, by displaying the very model of behavior, arouse our admiration to the point of boredom. Lope de Vega's work, on the other hand, is reminiscent of painting rather than sculpture. A vast canvas, now luminous now murky, on which all the figures shine with life and color, noblemen and commoners, archbishops and sea-captains, queens and country lasses, a restless, garrulous, exuberant, extravagant lot, madly swirling about like infusoria in a drop of water. To get a good view of the magnificent mass of the Spanish theater one must not open one's eyes wide as though following the pure line of a profile, but rather keep them half shut with a painter's gesture, with the gesture of Velázquez looking at the Meninas, the dwarfs, and the royal couple.

This point of view, it seems to me, affords the best angle under which to behold our theater today. The experts in Spanish literature—I know very little of it—ought to adopt it; it may prove fruitful and direct the analysis toward the true values of that immense poetical crop.

My purpose here was merely to oppose an art of figures to an art of adventures. For I have a notion that in our time the novel of high style must turn from the latter to the former. Instead of constructing interesting plots—which is practically impossible—it must invent interesting characters.

DOSTOEVSKI AND PROUST

⟮ While other great names are setting, carried down into oblivion by the mysterious revolution of the times, that of Dostoevski has established itself firmly in the zenith. Perhaps the present fervent admiration of his work is a trifle exaggerated, and I would rather reserve my judgment for a serener hour. At any rate, he has escaped from the general shipwreck of nineteenth century novels. But the reasons usually given to explain his triumph and his ability to survive seem to me erroneous. The interest his novels arouse is attributed to their material: the mysteriously dramatic action, the utterly pathological character of the personages, the exotic quality of those Slavic souls so different in their turbulent intricacy from our clear and neat dispositions. All this may contribute to the pleasure we draw from Dostoevski; only it is not sufficient reason. Moreover, there is a certain questionable quality to these features that makes them as well suited to repelling as to attracting us. We remember that those novels used to leave us with a mingled feeling of pleasure and uneasy confusion.

The material never saves a work of art, the gold it is made of does not hallow a statue. A work of art lives on its form, not on its material; the essential grace it emanates springs from its structure, from its organism. The structure forms the properly artistic part of the work, and on it aesthetic and literary criticism should concentrate. If too much stress is laid on the subject of a painting or a poem, sensitive nerves smell the Philistine. No doubt, as there is no life without chemical processes, thus there is no work of art without a subject. Just as life cannot be reduced to chemistry but begins to be life only when it has imposed upon the chemical laws other original processes of a new and more complex order, so the work of art is what it is thanks to the form it imposes upon the material or subject.

I have often wondered why even experts find it difficult to recognize that form, which to the uninitiated may seem abstract and inefficient, is the true substance of art. The author's or the critic's point of view cannot be the same as that of the unqualified reader who is concerned exclusively with the ultimate and total effect the work has on him and does not care to analyze the genesis of his pleasure.

As it is, much has been said about what is going on in Dostoevski's novels and very little about their form. The extraordinary quality of the events and emotions this formidable writer describes has fascinated the critics and prevented them from penetrating into what, at first sight, seems accidental and extrinsic but in reality forms the essence of the work: the structure of the novel as such. Hence a curious optical delusion. The turbulent, wayward character of his personages is ascribed to Dostoevski himself, and the novelist is looked upon as one more figure in his own novels—which indeed seem begotten in an hour of demoniacal ecstasy by some nameless elemental power, akin to the thunder and brother of the winds.

But all this is mere fancy. An alert mind may indulge in such colorful pictures but will soon dismiss them for the sake of clear ideas. It may be that the man Dostoevski was a poor epileptic or, if one so desires, a prophet. But the novelist Dostoevski was an *homme de lettres*, a conscientious craftsman of a sublime craft, and nothing else. Many a time have I tried in vain to convince Pío Baroja that Dostoevski was, above all, a past master of novelistic technique and one of the greatest innovators of the form of the novel.

There is no better example of what I have called the sluggish character of the genre. Dostoevski's books are almost all extremely long. But the story that is told is usually quite short. Sometimes it takes two volumes to describe what happens in three days, indeed, in a few hours. And yet, is there anything more intense? It is an error to believe that intensity is achieved through an accumulation of occurrences. Just the opposite; the fewer the better, providing they are detailed, i.e., "realized." Here, as in many other instances, the *multum non multa* applies. Density is obtained not by piling adventure upon adventure but by drawing out each incident through a copious presentation of its minutest components.

The concentration of the plot in time and space, so characteristic of Dostoevski's technique, brings to mind, in an unexpected sense, the venerable unities of classical tragedy. This aesthetic rule, which calls for moderation and restraint, now appears as an efficient means of bringing about the inner density, the high pressure, as it were, within the body of the novel.

Dostoevski never tires of filling pages and pages with the unending conversations of his personages. Thanks to this abundant flow of words the imaginary persons acquire a palpable bodily existence such as no definition could contrive.

It is extremely interesting to watch Dostoevski in his cunning ways with the reader. To a perfunctory observation, he seems to define each of his personages. When he introduces a figure he nearly always begins by briefly giving a biography of that person and thus makes us believe that we know well enough with what kind of man we are dealing. But no sooner do his people begin to act—i.e., to talk and to do things—than we feel thrown off the track. They refuse to behave according to those alleged definitions. The first conceptual image we were given of them is followed by another in which we see their immediate life, independent of the author's definition; and the two do not tally. At this point, the reader, afraid to lose sight of the personages at the crossroads of these contradictory data, sets forth in their pursuit by trying to reconcile the discrepant facts to make a unified picture. That is, he gets busy to find a definition himself. Now this is what we are doing in our living intercourse with people. Chance leads them into the ambit of our life, and nobody bothers officially to define them to us. What we have before us is their intricate reality not their plain concept. We are never quite let into their secret, they stubbornly refuse to adjust themselves to our ideas about them. And this is what makes them independent of us and brings it home that they are an effective reality transcending our imagination. But is not then Dostoevski's "realism"—let us call it that not to complicate things—not so much a matter of the persons and events he presents as of the way the reader sees himself compelled to deal with these persons and events? Dostoevski is a "realist" not because he uses the material of life but because he uses the form of life.

In this ruse of laying false scent Dostoevski indulges to the degree of cruelty. Not only does he refuse clearly to define his figures beforehand, but as their behavior varies from stage to stage they display one facet after another and thus seem to be shaped and assembled step by step before our eyes. Instead of stylizing the characters Dostoevski is pleased to have their ambiguity appear as unmitigatedly as in real life. And the reader, proceeding by trial and error, apprehensive all the time of making a mistake, must work out as best he can the actual character of those fickle creatures.

Owing to this device, among others, Dostoevski's

books, whatever their other qualities, have the rare virtue of never appearing sham and conventional. The reader never stumbles upon theatrical props; he feels from the outset immersed in a sound and effective quasi-reality. For a novel, in contrast to other literary works, must, while it is read, not be conceived as a novel; the reader must not be conscious of curtain and stage-lights. Reading Balzac, for example, we are on every page thrown out of the dream-world of the novel because we have bumped into the novelistic scaffolding. However, the most important structural peculiarity of Dostoevski's novels is harder to explain; I will return to it later.

But let me here add that this habit of confusing instead of defining, this condensation of time and space, in brief, this sluggishness or *tempo lento* are not peculiar to Dostoevski alone. All novels that are still readable employ more or less the same methods. As a West European example we may mention all the great books of Stendhal. *Le rouge et le noir*, a biographical novel which relates a few years of a man's life, is composed in the form of three or four pictures, each proceeding within its bounds like an entire novel of the Russian master.

In the last great example of prose narrative— Proust's colossal work—this inner structure becomes even more manifest and is, in a way, carried to an extreme. So slowly does the action move that it seems more like a sequence of ecstatic stillnesses without progress or tension. Reading this "remembrance of things

past" we feel convinced that the permissible measure
of slowness is overstepped. Plot there is almost none;
and not a whit of dramatic interest. Thus the novel is
reduced to pure motionless description, and the diffuse,
atmospheric character, which is in fact essential to the
genre, appears here with exaggerated purity. We feel
the lack of a firm and rigid support, of something like
the ribs in an umbrella. Deprived of its bones, the body
of the novel is converted into a cloudy, shapeless mass.
That is why I have said before that action and plot may
play a minor part in a modern novel, but that they cannot be entirely dispensed with. They fulfill the same
function—a mechanical function, it is true—as the
string of a necklace, the ribs of an umbrella, the poles
of a tent.

My thesis is that in the novel the so-called dramatic
interest has no aesthetic value but forms a mechanical
necessity. The reason for this necessity is to be found in
a general law of the human soul which deserves a brief
exposition.

ACTION AND CONTEMPLATION

❮ More than ten years ago I pointed out in my book
*Meditaciones del Quijote** that it is the essential task of
the modern novel to describe an atmosphere while other
narrative literary forms—epics, romances of chivalry,
adventure stories, dime novels, serials—relate concrete

* *Meditaciones del Quijote.* Madrid: Calpe, 1913.

and clearly outlined actions. Compared with a concrete action, which moves as fast as possible toward a conclusion, atmosphere signifies something diffuse and at rest. Action carries us away in its dramatic course; atmosphere invites to contemplation. In painting, a landscape has an atmospheric theme in which "nothing happens"; a battle piece narrates an isolated, well-defined event. It is not by chance that the technique of *plain air*—that is, of atmosphere—was invented in connection with landscape painting.

As time passes, my first impression has been confirmed. The taste of the best readers and the intent of the best writers have made it increasingly clear that the novel is destined to be a diffuse genre, and the latest creation of high art in the field of narrative prose, Proust's work, has given a decisive proof by overstressing the nondramatic character of the novel. Proust radically foregoes carrying the reader away through the dynamism of an intrigue and leaves him in a purely contemplative attitude. But it is this radicalism that is to blame for the difficulties and disappointments we experience in reading Proust. At the foot of each page we would implore the author to let us have a little dramatic interest, well though we know that not this but what he gives us so abundantly is the truly delicious fare. What he gives us is a microscopic analysis of human souls. With a pinch of drama—really, we should have been satisfied with almost nothing—the work would have been perfect.

How is this to be explained? Why do we find it difficult to read a novel which we appreciate unless we are accorded a minimum of action which we do not appreciate? I feel certain that anyone who gives some thought to the pleasure he derives from reading the great novels of literature will come upon this same puzzle.

That something is indispensable for something else does not imply that it is in itself estimable. To reveal a crime an informer may be needed, but that does not exonerate the informer.

Enjoyment of art is something that occurs in the mind when one sees a painting or reads a book. In order that this pleasure may be produced the psychic mechanism must function in a certain way, and all the prerequisites for this functioning must be present in the work of art although they may possess no aesthetic value or only a reflected and secondary one. In a novel, I would say, dramatic interest is a psychological necessity—not more, but not less either. But this is not the accepted belief. A suggestive plot is generally regarded as one of the decisive aesthetic factors of which there cannot be too much in a novel. Whereas I believe that action, as it is a merely mechanical element and aesthetically dead weight, ought to be reduced to a minimum. But at the same time, and with a view to Proust, I should consider this minimum indispensable.

The question transcends the range of the novel and even that of art in general and acquires major importance in philosophy. It deals with nothing less than the antagonism between action and contemplation. Two types of men become discernible: one inclined to pure contemplation, the other eager to act, to have a hand in things, to be involved emotionally. What things are can be ascertained by contemplation only. Interest beclouds contemplation; it induces us to take sides and blinds us to certain things while throwing others into undue relief. Science, resolved to do nothing but faithfully reflect the multiform face of the cosmos, adopts, from the outset, a contemplative attitude. Similarly, art is an enjoyment of contemplation.

Contemplation and interest thus appear to be two polar forms of consciousness which in principle exclude one another. A man of action is likely to be a poor thinker, if a thinker at all, while the ideal of the sage, the stoic for instance, is to live detached and to keep his soul motionless like a still lake which impassively mirrors the fleeting skies.

But such a radical contrast is, like all radicalism, a construction of the geometrical spirit. Pure contemplation does not exist and cannot exist. When we stand before the universe unmoved by any personal interest we see nothing well. For the things equally worth seeing are innumerable. No reason speaks for our focusing on one point in preference to another, and our eyes wander aimlessly over an amorphous landscape without order or perspective. It is a humble and hackneyed truth that in order to see one must look and in order to look one must pay attention. Attention is a preference subjectively bestowed upon some things at the cost of others. I cannot focus on the first without losing sight of the second. Attention is like a ray of light which illuminates a zone of objects and creates a penumbra around it.

Pure contemplation claims to be rigorously impartial. The spectacle of the world is taken in without any intervention and distortion on the part of the subject. But at the back of contemplation, as an indispensable presupposition, we now discern functioning the mechanism of attention which directs the eye from within the subject and throws things into perspective according to a value pattern originating in the inner recesses of the person. It is not that attention is given to what is seen but, on the contrary, only what attracts attention is seen well. Attention is a psychological a priori that operates by means of affective preferences, i.e., interests.

Modern psychology has found itself compelled paradoxically to reverse the traditional order of mental faculties. Scholasticism taught: *ignoti nulla cupido*—what is unknown is not desired. The truth is rather the opposite: Only that which has been in some way desired or, to be exact, which has previously aroused interest, is known well. How it is possible to be interested in what is not yet known presents a problem I have tried to solve in my essay "Iniciación en la estimativa."*

I cannot now enter upon a subject of such scope. Let everybody look in his own past for the circumstances under which he learned most about the world, and he will find that it was not when he deliberately set himself to seeing and nothing but seeing. It is not the countryside we visited as sightseers that we know best. Tourists,

* Cf. *Revista de Occidente,* No. IV.

although exclusively preoccupied with observing and thus in a position to carry home the richest booty of knowledge, are known to gather superficial information; their contact with a city or a country is not intimate enough to reveal the peculiar conditions. Peasants, on the other hand, whose relation to the land is one of pure interest, are apt to betray, as anyone who has traveled in rural districts will know, an amazing ignorance of their own country. Of all that surrounds them they know only such things as bear directly on their agricultural concerns.

This indicates that the most favorable position for gathering knowledge—that is, for absorbing the largest number and the best quality of objective data—lies somewhere in between pure contemplation and pressing interest. Some vital interests that are not too narrow and oppressive are required for organizing our contemplation; they must limit and articulate it by imposing upon it a perspective of attention. With respect to the countryside the hunter that hunts for sport may, *coeteris paribus*, be said to know a region best and to come into most profitable touch with all the manifold sides of the terrain. As to cities, we have seen none so well as those in which we lived in love. Love, in gathering all our soul around its delightful object, endowed us with a keener sensibility that took in the environment without making it the deliberate center of vision.

The paintings that have impressed us most are not those of museums we visited "to look at pictures" but may be humble pieces beheld in the twilight of a room where life led us on very different purposes. In a concert a piece of music falls flat that, when a blind man plays it in the street, may move our heart.

It is evident that man's destiny is not primarily contemplative; hence the best condition for contemplation cannot be to make it a directly intended, primary act. Only when it is confined to a secondary part, while the soul is moved by the dynamism of an interest, does our perceiving and absorbing power reach a maximum.

If this were not so, the first man who looked at the universe would have beheld it in its entirety. But as it happens, mankind is discovering the world bit by bit in ever-widening circles—as though each of the vital human situations, each urge, need, and interest had served as a perceptive organ with which to explore a small neighborhood.

Hence it appears that those elements which seem to disturb pure contemplation—interests, sentiments, compulsions, affective preferences—are precisely its indispensable instruments. Any human destiny that does not labor under an unbearable strain can become a tower of contemplation—an observatory—of such scope that none, not even a seemingly more privileged one, can replace it. Thus the humblest and most wretched life is capable of receiving a theoretical sanctification and an untransferable mission of wisdom—although only certain types of existence are possessed of the optimum conditions required for attaining to the highest grades of knowledge.

But enough of generalities. Let us merely keep in

mind that there has to be at least a dash of action to make contemplation possible. Since the world of the novel is imaginary the author must mobilize in us some imaginary interest, a bit of excitement that gives our faculty of perceiving a certain guidance and a dynamic support. The reader's thirst for dramatic action has subsided with the sharpening of his psychological insight; and this is fortunate, for present-day novelists are at a loss to invent great new plots. As I see it, they need not be upset. A bit of movement and tension will do. But this bit is indispensable. Proust has demonstrated the necessity of movement by writing a paralytic novel.

THE NOVEL AS "PROVINCIAL LIFE"

❲ Hence the order must be inverted: the action or plot is not the substance of a novel but its scaffolding, its mechanical prop. The essence of the novel—that is to say, of the modern novel with which alone I am here concerned—does not lie in "what happens" but precisely in the opposite: in the personages' pure living, in their being and being thus, above all, in the ensuing milieu. Indirect proof of this may be found in the fact that of the best novels we are liable to remember not the events, not what befalls the personages but only the personages themselves. The titles of certain books are like names of cities in which we used to live for a time. They at once bring back a climate, a peculiar smell of streets, a general type of people and a specific rhythm of life.

Only then, if at all, some particular scene may come to mind.

Indeed, novelists need not strain to build up an action. Any one serves the purpose. As a classical example of how independent a novel is of the plot I have always regarded a work of Stendhal's which he left less than half finished and which has been published under different titles: *Lucien Leuwen, Le chasseur vert*, etc. The existing part amounts to a considerable number of pages. Yet nothing happens in it. A young officer comes to the capital of a *départment* and falls in love with a lady who belongs to the provincial aristocracy. We witness in minute detail the development of this delightful sentiment in the two persons: that is all. When the action begins to become involved, the fragment ends. But it leaves us with the impression that we could have gone on forever reading page after page about life in that corner of France, about the lady of the legitimist party and the young soldier in his amaranthine uniform.

And what else is needed? Above all, let us pause to think what this "else" could be—those "interesting things," those marvelous experiences. In the realm of the novel nothing of the kind exists (we do not now speak of serials or of scientific adventure stories in the manner of Poe, Wells, etc.); here life is precisely daily life. It is in reporting the wonders of the simple, unhaloed hour, not in expatiating on the extraordinary, that the novel displays its specific graces.* Not by wid-

* This aesthetic stress on the daily and this strict preclusion of marvels and wonders is essential to the modern novel. It charac-

ening our horizon with tales of unheard-of adventures can the novelist expect to captivate us. The opposite procedure is required: the reader's horizon must be narrowed. Let me explain.

If by horizon we understand the circle of people and events that integrate the world of each of us, we may be misled into believing that certain horizons are so wide and varied that they are particularly interesting while others are too narrow and monotonous to command interest. In point of fact, the duchess whose world seems so dramatic to a young secretary is liable to be quite as bored in her glamorous sphere as the romantic typist in her drab and obscure environment. Being a duchess is as daily a form of life as any other.

The truth is that no horizon is especially interesting by itself, by virtue of its peculiar content, and that any horizon, wide or narrow, brilliant or dull, varied or monotonous, may possess an interest of its own which merely requires a vital adjustment to be discovered. Human vitality is so exuberant that in the sorriest desert it still finds a pretext for glowing and trembling. Living in the city we cannot understand how it is possible to exist in the village. But no sooner has some chance landed us there than we find ourselves vehemently taking sides in the local gossip.

In my judgment, this is of paramount importance to

terizes *Don Quixote* in contrast to the romances of chivalry. Indeed, were we to determine the conditions of the modern novel, we should only need to ascertain what a literary prose production must look like that makes a principle of eliminating marvels.

the novel. The author must see to it that the reader is cut off from his real horizon and imprisoned in a small, hermetically sealed universe—the inner realm of the novel. He must make a "villager" of him and interest him in the inhabitants of this realm. For, however admirable these may be, they cannot hold their own against the beings of flesh and bone who form the reader's daily surroundings and constantly claim his interest. To turn each reader into a temporal "provincial" is the great secret of the novelist. Instead of widening the horizon— what novelistic horizon could be wider and richer than the humblest real one?—he must contract and limit it. Thus and only thus can he make the reader care about what is going on inside the novel.

No horizon, I repeat, is interesting for its content. Any one of them is interesting through its *form*—its form as a horizon, that is, as a cosmos or complete world. Microcosm and macrocosm are equally cosmos; they differ only in the size of their radii; but for a being that lives inside, each has a constant absolute size. We are reminded of Poincaré's remark—which foreshadows the theory of relativity—that, if everything in our world contracted and shrank in the same proportion, we should not notice the difference.

The interdependence between horizon and interest— that each horizon has its interest—is the vital law thanks to which in the aesthetic field the novel is possible.

From this law derive a few norms of the genre.

IMPERVIOUSNESS

❨ Let us observe ourselves the moment we have finished reading a great novel. Is it not as though we were emerging from another world where we were held incommunicado? That there can have been no communication is clear; for we are aware of no transition. A second ago we were in Parma with Count Mosca and La Sanseverina, with Clélia and Fabrice; we lived their lives with them, immersed in their atmosphere, their time and place. Now, abruptly, we find ourselves in our room, our city, our time; and already our accustomed preoccupations begin to stir. There is an interval of indecision and suspense. Perchance a sudden wave of recollection washes us back into the universe of the novel, and with a certain effort, as though struggling through a liquid element, we must regain the shores of our existence proper. Were someone to find us in just that moment, our dilated pupils would betray our shipwrecked condition.

Novel I call the literary prose work that produces this effect. And a novel that lacks this glorious and unique magic is a poor novel whatever other virtues it may possess. Sublime and beneficent the power of this sovereign modern art that multiplies our existence, freeing us from our own self and generously bestowing upon us the gift of transmigration!

To achieve this, the author must begin by luring us into the closed precinct that is his novel and then keep us there cut off from any possible retreat to the real space we left behind. The first is easy; almost any promise finds us ready to enter through the gate the novelist holds open for us. The second is more difficult. The author must build around us a wall without chinks or loopholes through which we might catch, from within the novel, a glimpse of the outside world. For were we allowed to compare the inner world of the book with outer reality and invited to "live," the conflicts, problems, and emotions the book has to offer would seem so small and futile that all their significance would be lost. It would be like looking in a garden at a picture representing a garden. The painted garden blooms only inside a house against the neutral background of a wall where it is like a window opening into an imaginary noonday world.

In my judgment, no writer can be called a novelist unless he possesses the gift of forgetting, and thereby making us forget, the reality beyond the walls of his novel. Let him be as realistic as can be; that is to say, let the microcosm of his novel consist of unquestionably true-to-life elements—he will have lost out if he cannot keep us from remembering that there exists an extramural world.

Hence every novel is still-born that is laden with transcendental intentions, be they political, ideological, symbolical, or satirical. For those themes are of such a nature that they cannot be dealt with fictitiously, they have meaning only in relation to the actual horizon of each individual. As soon as they are broached we feel expelled from the imaginary sphere of the novel and compelled to establish contact with the absolute realm on which our real existence depends. How can we care about the imaginary destinies of his personages when the author forces us to face the acute problem of our own political or metaphysical destiny? No, he must by all means render us insensible to reality and keep up the hypnosis in which we lead an imaginary life.

This seems to me the cause of the enormous difficulty—if not impossibility—of writing a good historical novel. The aspiration that the imagined cosmos shall at the same time be historically correct leads to a perpetual clash between two different horizons. And since each horizon calls for a special adjustment of our perceptive apparatus we must constantly change our attitude. No opportunity is given us of either quietly dreaming the novel or clearly thinking the historical facts. Again and again we pause, uncertain whether to hold the events and characters against the imaginary or the historical horizon, and this ambivalence imparts a false and uncomfortable complexion to everything. Any attempt to merge the two worlds only leads to their mutual annihilation. The author, we feel, falsifies the historical facts by bringing them too near to us and weakens the novel by removing it too far away from us toward the abstract plane of historical truth.

Imperviousness is but the special form taken on in the novel by the generic imperative of art: to be without transcending consequence. This self-sufficiency of art cannot but irritate all muddleheads. But what are we to do about it, since after an inexorable law everything must be what it is and renounce being something else? There are people who want to be everything. Not content with being artists they want to be politicians and lead the multitude, or to be prophets entrusted with administering the will of God and guiding the consciences of men. But the arts take their revenge on any artist who wants to be more than an artist by letting his work fail even artistically. Conversely, a poet's politics rarely attain to more than an ingenuous, inept gesture.

By virtue of a purely aesthetic necessity the novel must be impervious, it must possess the power of forming a precinct, hermetically closed to all actual reality. From this condition there follows, among many other consequences, that the novel cannot propagate philosophical, political, sociological, or moral ideas; it can be nothing beyond a novel. As little can its inside transcend into any outside as a sleeper's arm can reach out into the waking world to catch a real object and introduce it into the magic sphere of his dream. The sleeper's arm is a phantom, too limp to lift a petal. So incompatible are the two worlds that their slightest contact abolishes one of them. As children we never could stick a finger through the shimmering skin of the soap bubbles; always those frail, floating globes would vanish in a sudden explosion, leaving a tear of foam on the flags.

This does by no means preclude that a novel, once it has been "lived" in a delightful sleep-walking way, may afterwards evoke in us all sorts of vital repercussions. The symbolical meaning of *Don Quixote* is not contained within the novel, we construct it from without when musing over our impressions of the book. Dostoevski's religious and political ideas are not operative agencies within the body of his work; they appear there with the same fictitious character as the faces and the frenetic passions of the figures.

Let all novelists look at the doors of the Florentine baptistery wrought by Lorenzo Ghiberti! In a series of small squares they show the whole Creation: men, women, animals, fruits, buildings. The sculptor was concerned with nothing but to model all those forms one after another. We still seem to feel the trembling delight with which the hand set down the arched brow of the ram Abraham espied in the thicket, and the plump form of the apple, and the foreshortened edifice. Similarly, a novelist must be inspired above all by a wonderful enthusiasm to tell a tale and to invent men and women and conversations and passions. A silkworm enclosed in his magic cocoon, he must forget the world he leaves behind and happily go about polishing the walls of his self-made prison so as to stop up all pores against the air and light of reality.

In simpler words, a novelist while he writes his novel must care more about his imaginary world than about any other possible world. If he does not care, how can he make us care? Somnambulist himself, he must infect us with his divine somnambulism.

❨ What I have called the impervious or hermetic character of the novel will be further elucidated by a comparison between the novel and the lyrical poem. We admire a poem when we see it rising miraculously from reality, as the artificial jet of a fountain rises from the surrounding scenery. Poems are made to be looked at from without—the same as statues, the same as Greek temples. They do not interfere with our daily world, or rather, they derive their peculiar grace from establishing amid our reality their naked unreality with Olympian innocence. Whereas the novel is destined to be perceived from within itself—the same as the real world in which, by inexorable metaphysical order, each man forms, in each moment of his life, the center of his own universe. To enjoy a novel we must feel surrounded by it on all sides; it cannot exist as a more or less conspicuous thing among the rest of things. Precisely because it is a preeminently realistic genre it is incompatible with outer reality. In order to establish its own inner world it must dislodge and abolish the surrounding one.

From this imperative derive all the other conditions of the novelistic form that we have pointed out. They all fall under the heading of imperviousness. Thus the imperative of autopsy follows inevitably from the fact that the novelist finds himself compelled to cover the real world with his imaginary world. If we are not to see a thing, if a thing is to be concealed, we must be shown other things that conceal it. But shades are known to

cast no shadow and not to screen from sight what is behind them—by these two tokens the dead in purgatory
recognize Dante as a trespasser from the land of the
living. Instead of defining his figures and their sentiments, the novelist must therefore evoke them in order
that their self-presence may intercept our vision of the
real world about us.

Now, as far as I can see, there is no other way of
achieving this but by supplying a wealth of detail. The
reader must be caught in a dense web of innumerable
minutely told circumstances. What is our life but an
immense agglomeration of trifles?

Since exaggeration always serves to call our attention
to the thing in its rightful measure, Proust's work, by
overdoing the prolixity and minuteness, has helped us
to recognize that great novels are essentially lavish of
particulars. Indeed, the books of Cervantes, Stendhal,
Dickens, Dostoevski are of the tightly packed sort. All
the time we are getting more facts than we can possibly
keep in mind, and yet we are left with the impression
that beyond those explicitly mentioned others are present potentially, as it were. Great novels are atolls built
by myriads of tiny animals whose seeming frailness
checks the impact of the seas.

For this reason a novelist should never attack a subject unless he knows it thoroughly. He must produce *ex
abundantia*. Where he finds himself moving in shallow
waters he will never make good.

Things must be accepted as they are. The novel is
not a lithe, agile, winged form. It is not for nothing that

all the great novels that we now like best are a bit heavy. The poet may set forth, a wandering minstrel, with his lyre under his arm, but the novelist moves with cumbrous baggage like circuses or nomadic tribes. He carries the furnishings of a whole world on his back.

DECLINE AND PERFECTION

(The conditions so far mentioned merely define the level at which the novel begins; they mark the water-line, as it were, of its continent. In the following we shall be concerned with conditions that determine the higher or lower altitude of a work.

The stuff novels are made of may vary a good deal. It may consist in trite and hackneyed observations, such as an average man uses for the purpose of his existence; or it may contain experiences for which one must probe deep into the secrets of the soul. The quality of the detail is among the factors that decide the rank of a book. The great novelist, contemptuous of the surface features of his personages, dives down into their souls and returns, clutching in his hand the deep-sea pearl. But precisely for this reason the average reader does not understand him.

In the beginnings of the novel the difference between good novels and poor novels was not so great. As nothing had yet been said they all had to begin with saying the obvious. Today, in the great hour of the decline of the genre, good novels and poor ones differ very much indeed. Hence the opportunity of achieving the perfect work is excellent—though extremely precarious. For it would be rash to assume that the season of decline is unfavorable in every respect. Rather, the works of highest rank are likely to be products of the last hour when accumulated experience has utterly refined the artistic sensitivity. The decline of an artistic genre, like that of a race, affects but the average specimens.

This is one of the reasons why I believe—utterly pessimistic though I feel about the immediate future of the plastic arts and of politics, though not of science or of philosophy—that the novel is one of the few fields that may still yield illustrious fruits, more exquisite ones perhaps than were ever garnered in previous harvests. As a routine production, as an exploitable mine, the novel may be finished. The large veins, accessible to any diligent hand, are worked out. What remains are hidden deposits and perilous ventures into the depths where, perchance, the most precious crystals grow. But that is work for minds of rare distinction.

The last perfection, almost always the fruit of the last hour, has not yet been attained by the novel. Neither its form or structure nor its material has passed through the last crucibles. Regarding the material I find some reason for optimism in the following consideration.

The material proper of the novel is imaginary psychology. Imaginary psychology advances in unison with scientific psychology and psychological intuition which is used in daily life. Now, few things have progressed so much in Europe these last fifty years as the knowledge of the human soul. For the first time in history there exists a science of psychology, in its beginnings only, it is true, but even so without equal in former ages. Add to this a refined ability of divining our neighbor and analyzing our own inner life. All this psychological knowledge accumulated in the contemporary mind through research or through spontaneous experience is to no small degree responsible for the present failure of the novel. Authors that yesterday seemed excellent appear naïve today because the present reader is a much better psychologist than the old author. (Who knows whether the political confusion in Europe, which to my mind is much more alarming and deep-seated than is now apparent, does not spring from the same causes? Who knows whether States of the modern type are not possible only while the citizens live in a state of psychological dumbness?)

A related phenomenon is the dissatisfaction we feel when reading the classical historians. The psychology they use seems inadequate and vague and far from satisfying our apparently subtler taste.*

Novelists and historians will hardly fail to make use of this progress of psychology. Humanity has always satisfied its desires if they were clear and concrete. Thus it is fairly safe to predict that—apart from philosophy—history and the novel will furnish the strongest intellectual emotions the near future holds in reserve for us.

* Cf. for this point the author's essay "Las Atlántidas" in his collected works: *Obras* (Espasa Calpe, 1932), II, 821.

❨ These notes on the novel have so resolutely an air of being interminable that it becomes necessary to cut them short. One more step would prove fatal. So far they have moved on a plane of ample generality, avoiding entanglements in casuistry. But in aesthetics, the same as in ethics, the general principles form but a system of reference set down with a view to the concrete analysis of special cases. It is with this analysis that the most appealing part of the investigation commences; but with it we also venture into a field without bounds. Thus prudence suggests that I stop here. —I would, however, add one last remark.

The material of the novel, we were saying, is, above all, imaginary psychology. It is not easy to explain in a few words what this means. The current belief is that psychological phenomena, like the phenomena of experimental physics, obey factual laws. If this is so, all the novelist can do is to observe and to copy the real processes in existing souls. But he cannot invent psychological processes and construct souls as the mathematician constructs geometrical figures. Yet the enjoyment of novels presupposes exactly this.

When a novelist expounds a psychological process he does not expect us to accept it as something that has actually happened—who would guarantee its reality? —but he trusts that it possesses an inner evidence, an evidence akin to that which makes mathematics possible. And let it not be said that the psychological development he describes seems convincing when it coincides with cases we have witnessed in life. An awkward thing it would be if the novelist had to rely on the chance experiences of this or that reader of his. Rather we recall that one of the peculiar attractions Dostoevski's work used to hold for us lay in the unfamiliar behavior of his personages. Small chance there is indeed that a reader in Sevilla should ever in his life have met people as chaotic and turbulent as the Karamasoffs. And yet, dull though he may be, the psychic mechanism of those souls seems to him as cogent and evident as the steps of a mathematical proof which uses dimensions never seen by human eyes.

There exists in psychology, just as in mathematics, an evidence a priori. Because of this in either field imaginary construction is possible. Where only facts are subject to laws but no laws obtain that regulate the imagination it is impossible to construct. Any attempt to do so can be no more than an arbitrary caprice.

Because this is not recognized the psychology in a novel is taken to be identical with that of real life, and it is assumed that the author can do nothing but copy reality. So coarse a reasoning lies at the bottom of what is currently called "realism." I cannot now discuss this involved term which I have been careful always to use in quotation marks to render it suspect. Its incongruity will clearly transpire when we observe that it does not even apply to the very works from which it allegedly derives. The personages of those works are almost all of them so different from those we meet in our own environment that, even supposing they were copied from existing persons, we should not recognize them as such. People in a novel need not be like real ones, it is enough that they are possible. And this psychology of possible human minds, which I have called imaginary psychology, is the only one that matters to the novel. That a novel may, apart from this, be concerned with giving a psychological interpretation of actual social types and environments can provide an additional piquancy, but it is not essential. (One of the points I am leaving untouched is that the novel lends itself more easily than any other literary form to absorbing elements alien to art. *Within* the novel almost anything fits: science, religion, sociology, aesthetic criticism—if only it is ultimately derealized and confined within the inner world of the novel; i.e., if it remains without actual and effective validity. In other words, a novel can contain as much sociology as it desires, but the novel itself cannot be sociological. The dose of alien elements a book can bear, lastly, depends on the author's capability of dissolving them in the atmosphere of the novel as such. But this subject obviously belongs to casuistry, and I drop it terrified.)

This possibility of constructing human souls is perhaps the major asset of future novels. Everything points in this direction. The interest in the outer mechanism of the plot is today reduced to a minimum. All the better: the novel must now revolve about the superior interest emanating from the inner mechanism of the personages. Not in the invention of plots but in the invention of interesting characters lies the best hope of the novel.